JOHN GOWER'S LITERARY TRANSFORMATIONS IN THE CONFESSIO AMANTIS

Original Articles and Translations

W9-CDK-711

Edited by

Peter G. Beidler

Lehigh University

Contributors:

Peter G. Beidler
Edna S. deAngeli
Patricia Innerbichler De Bellis
Carole Koepke Brown
Natalie Epinger Ruyak
John B. Gaston
Douglas L. Lepley
Judith C. G. Moran
Nicolette Stasko
Karl A. Zipf, Jr.

UNIVERSITY
PRESS OF
AMERICA

Library of Congress Cataloging in Publication Data
Main entry under title:

John Gower's literary transformations in the Confessio
    amantis.

    Includes bibliographical references.
    1. Gower, John, 1325?-1408. Confessio amantis--
Sources. 2. Ovid, 43 B.C.-17 or 18. Metamorphoses.
3. Ovid, 43 B.C.-17 or 18--Influence--Gower.
4. Alexander, the Great, 356-323 B.C.--Romances--
History and criticism. I. Gower, John, 1325?-1408.
II. Beidler, Peter G. III. Title.
PR1984.C63J6 1982   821'.1   81-40599
ISBN 0-8191-2596-2
ISBN 0-8191-2597-0 (pbk.)

To the professors and students of the
Lehigh University English Department.

TABLE OF CONTENTS

TABLE OF CONTENTS continued

PREFACE

Most of the first part of this book was written by graduate students I have had the pleasure of teaching in the past several years at Lehigh University in my course on Middle English Literature. It grew out of my conviction that students can do real scholarship and make real discoveries if given the chance. Rather than have them write those traditional exercises called "term papers," I encouraged them to work on real problems in literary criticism. One such problem was to understand the kind of stories which John Gower, Chaucer's contemporary and fellow poet, had written for the _Confessio Amantis_. Did Gower merely retell the classical narratives which were his favorite sources, or did he put his own distinctively medieval and personal stamp on them? If the latter, how might we best describe that stamp? I tried to show my students the way by writing a couple of essays on Gower's treatment of his sources, then turned them loose on their own Gower tales. Part One of this book, then, is a collection of the sixteen essays that resulted from those experiments in "hands-on" training in literary criticism.

The second part of the book focuses more narrowly on one of the stories in Gower's _Confessio Amantis_, the Tale of Nectanabus, which deals with the magical events surrounding the birth of Alexander the Great. Once again anxious to discover what kinds of changes Gower made as he adapted older stories to his own literary purposes, I decided to compare Gower's account of the birth of Alexander with those found in his sources-- particularly the Anglo-Norman _Roman de toute Chevalerie_. I asked Patricia De Bellis of Cedar Crest College if she would help me to translate certain key

vii

portions of the story. She responded, more fully than I had any right to expect that she might, with a complete translation. Later my colleague, Edna deAngeli of Lehigh University's Classics Department, kindly translated for me a Latin version of the same tale, Julius Valerius's <u>Res Gestae Alexandri Macedonis</u>. Although the Latin story was probably not a direct source for the Gower tale, it provides many interesting parallels. Having used those translations for my own purposes, I thought it wasteful to deprive other potential users direct access to them. Part Two of this book, then, consists of my own essay on the originality of Gower's tale, followed by the texts of the two works with the translations on facing pages.

Our conclusions in both parts are clear. John Gower wrote with great originality and clear purpose in adapting to his own literary needs the stories of older writers.

We wish to express our gratitude to the Lehigh University Office of Research for the funds which paid for most of the typing of the manuscript, to Loralee Choman for editorial assistance in preparing the manuscript for publication, and to Beatrice Buck and Lori Heinly for their careful and expert typing.

P.G.B.

PART ONE

Gower's Metamorphosis of Ovid's <u>Metamorphoses</u>

Introduction to Part One

It is unfortunate that John Gower's Middle English
works have always been compared with the unquestionably
more appealing ones of Geoffrey Chaucer. Such
comparisons, if they tell anything about Gower's work,
tell far more about what it is <u>not</u> than about what it
is. The comparisons seem to demonstrate that Gower's
work is not humorous, that it does not have great
variety of tone, that it does not set forth many
realistic characters, and even that it is not
"artistic" by comparison with Chaucer's. We have no
desire to argue here with such judgments. We do feel,
however, that Gower, who in his lifetime and for some
centuries after was considered to be at least Chaucer's
equal, deserves more from us in the twentieth century
than to be read merely as a foil for Chaucer's
greatness. We propose in Part One to compare some of
Gower's tales in the <u>Confessio</u> <u>Amantis</u> not with stories
in the <u>Canterbury</u> <u>Tales</u>, but with ones in Ovid's
<u>Metamorphoses</u>, Gower's favorite source of story
materials.

Gower reworked for the <u>Confessio</u> <u>Amantis</u> many of
Ovid's stories from the <u>Metamorphoses</u>. Sometimes he
combined what he read there with what he read in one or
more other sources. In the present study, we have
selected for discussion those tales which Gower derives
almost exclusively from the <u>Metamorphoses</u>, for we want
to demonstrate as clearly as possible what changes
Gower was making and why he made them. We have not
been particularly interested in determining whether
Gower's tales are any "better" or any "worse" than
Ovid's; we have been interested, rather, in measuring
the degree of Gower's artistic independence from his
Ovidian sources, and in ascertaining what a comparison

of a Gower tale to its source reveals about Gower's intentions in adapting classical plots and characters to his own fourteenth-century literary needs.

Before we begin our anaylses of individual tales which Gower adapted from Ovid's _Metamorphoses_, we would like to summarize our findings. Whereas Ovid was interested primarily in telling a series of stories about transformations, Gower often plays down or eliminates altogether the transformation scene from his source. Gower's tales are almost always more explicitly moralistic and Christian than Ovid's; often, as a result, they are shorter, for Gower uses only those features of Ovid's stories which contribute directly to the point he is trying to make. Because Genius, the narrator of all of the tales in the _Confessio Amantis_, attempts to convey a clear moral rather than to tell a highly moving story, Gower's accounts tend to be more "tellings" than "dramatizations." Gower adapts his tales from Ovid to fit as neatly as possible into the moral framework of Amans' confession to Genius. For example, Gower alters tales in Liber Quartus, which focuses on the sin of sloth, to demonstrate as directly as possible a particular kind of sloth. For another example, distinctly minor Ovidian characters who demonstrated a vice which Gower wants to exemplify are sometimes raised to the level of main characters. Similarly, attractive characters are sometimes changed to unattractive and clearly sinful ones. And supernatural characters--gods, nymphs, monsters--are sometimes made human, while lower-class characters are sometimes transformed into knights or even princes, to make their situations as similar as possible to that of Amans.

In sum, Gower adopts selectively from Ovid, changes or eliminates what he cannot adopt directly, and invents entirely when he needs to. Far from being a slavish translator or an unoriginal reteller, Gower makes the stories he learned from Ovid his own fresh and remarkably controlled works of literature.

Although we have all profited from the suggestions and criticisms of others in the group, the author whose name follows the title of each chapter assumes full responsibility for the ideas in that section and for the way those ideas are presented. For the convenience of our readers, we have provided at the start of each section a brief summary of the plot of the Ovidian source for Gower's tale. One tale--the Tale of Tereus--has been the subject of previous extended source study (see Derek Pearsall, "Gower's Narrative Art," PMLA, 81 [1966], 478-79, and Bruce Harbert, "The Myth of Tereus in Ovid and Gower," MAE, 41 [1972], 208-14). For an extensive bibliography of scholarly discussions of Gower's works, see Robert F. Yeager, John Gower Materials: A Bibliography through 1979 (New York: Garland Publishing, Inc., 1981). All quotations from the Confessio Amantis are taken from G. C. Macaulay's The English Works of John Gower, volumes 1 and 2 (Oxford: Oxford University Press, 1900-1901). The quotations are given by book numbers. Thus, "V, 6752" refers to that line number in Liber Quintus, which appears in Macaulay's second volume.

The Tale of Acteon (CA, I, 333-78)

--Peter G. Beidler

Ovid's account of the death of Acteon (Metamorphoses, III, 138-252) is vivid and moving. One day, after a particularly bloody morning of hunting, Acteon tells his companions to put away their weapons and to hunt no more that day. Then Acteon wanders out alone to see the countryside. Through no fault of his own the fates direct his steps to a grove where the goddess Diana is bathing naked in the stream. When Acteon comes into the grove, Diana's nymphs cry out and gather closely around her so that Acteon sees nothing of her except her head and shoulders. Diana, however, is furious. To prevent Acteon from telling anyone that he has seen her undressed, she splashes him with water from the stream. The water transforms Acteon into a stag. Horns grow on his brow, his neck lengthens, his ears grow pointed, his hands become feet, his skin becomes a dappled hide. Acteon flees, but does not know where to run. Soon his hounds--over thirty of them are mentioned by name--see him and, encouraged by Acteon's hunting companions, pursue him. He tries to call out to them and tell them who he is, but, now a deer, he cannot make human sounds. Soon the hounds overtake the fleeing Acteon, bring him down, and savagely tear into him. His friends wish that Acteon were there to witness the glorious kill, not realizing that he is the deer. Only after Acteon dies from his innumerable wounds is Diana's anger appeased.

Gower vastly simplifies and shortens this dramatic story. Gone in Gower's version are Acteon's hunting companions and the catalogue of the names of the hounds. Gone is Acteon's decision to desist from

7

further hunting that day. Gone is the description of
the disrobing of Diana by her attendant nymphs. Gone
is the detailed account of her transformation of Acteon
into a deer. Gone are the extended chase by the
hounds, the detailed account of their killing of
Acteon, and Acteon's futile efforts to cry out and
identify himself. Indeed, Gower reduces the
transformation, the chase, and the kill--which occupied
some sixty lines in Ovid--to a mere nine lines:

> the liknesse
> Sche made him taken of an Hert,
> Which was tofore hise houndes stert,
> That ronne besiliche aboute
> With many an horn and many a route,
> That maden mochel noise and cry:
> And ate laste unhappely
> This Hert his oghne houndes slowhe
> And him for vengance al todrowhe.
> (I, 370-78)

In short, Gower appears to have taken Ovid's moving
narrative and reduced it to a bare plot outline lacking
intense drama and undermining sympathy for its main
character.

We must recall, however, that Gower's purpose in
telling about Acteon is neither to tell a dramatic
story nor to translate Ovid's fine account into Middle
English. Rather, Gower's purpose is to use the story
of Acteon to demonstrate the dangers of looking when
one should not look, the moral inappropriateness of
gazing upon the forbidden. For Gower, then, the tale
of Acteon becomes an "ensample touchende of mislok" (I,
334), and he consistently eliminates elements in Ovid's
tale, however vivid or dramatic they were, which would
not advance this moral purpose. The catalogue of the
names of the thirty-odd hounds, for example, or the
excitingly dramatized chase, would have done little to
convey Gower's theme about mislooking.

Not only does Gower eliminate unnecessary parts of
Ovid's tale, but he also invents a number of details
which help to advance his moral purpose. Probably the
most important single change Gower makes in his tale is
to transform Acteon from the highly sympathetic hero he
was in Ovid into the rather unsympathetic Peeping Tom
he is in the Confessio Amantis. One small but
important invention of Gower's is Acteon's pride.
Acteon, Gower tells us, "above alle othre caste his
chiere" (I, 341). There was no hint of haughtiness or

8

arrogance in Ovid's Acteon. Gower's suggestion of pride not only helps to fit this tale into Liber Primus, the subject of which is, of course, the first of the Seven Deadly Sins, but it also helps to show that Acteon is morally responsible for his own downfall. Far from suggesting that Acteon was in any sense guilty of sin or even of bad judgment, Ovid specifically exonerated Acteon by stating that his downfall was caused by destiny and not by guilt. If Gower's exemplum, however, is to have any force as a guide to the actions of Amans, it must lay at Acteon's own feet the responsibility for his terrible punishment.

To demonstrate further that Acteon brings about his own downfall, Gower also changes Ovid's tale by having Acteon actively hunting when he sees Diana. In Ovid, we recall, Acteon was merely out wandering after he had called off the hunt for the afternoon. Gower's minor change contributes to a sense of poetic justice when the prideful hunter becomes the desperate hunted by the end of the story. More important for the specific moral of his tale about the dangers of looking unwisely, Gower greatly alters the circumstances of Acteon's seeing of Diana. Ovid never quite stated that Acteon had even looked at the nude Diana. He did state that Diana's nude nymphs saw him and cried out in alarm to warn Diana. But even if Ovid's Acteon had looked directly at Diana, he would have seen nothing but her head and shoulders, for in Ovid's story the nymphs rushed to shield her body with their own as soon as they saw Acteon. In Gower's version, on the other hand, Acteon is said clearly to "caste his yhe" (I, 360) to the place where the goddess was bathing, and to "syh" (I, 361) where "Diana naked stod" (I, 363). There is no question that Acteon looks, and that he sees the goddess naked. Then, to further emphasize Acteon's responsibility, Gower tells us that Acteon does not look away after first seeing Diana: "Bot he his yhe awey ne swerveth/ Fro hire, which was naked al" (I, 366-67). Notice also this second emphasizing of Diana's unconcealed nakedness, for in Gower the nymphs are not aware of Acteon's looking before she herself is. They do not warn her of his presence, and they do not conceal her nakedness with their own bodies. Unlike his Ovidian counterpart, Gower's Acteon looks, rather than merely sees, looks at an unconcealed nude Diana, and then continues to look at her.

In short, Gower makes the story of Acteon his own. He takes a narrative which demonstrated the ill effects

9

of a hero's accidentally incurring the unreasonable
fury of Diana, and transforms it into one which
demonstrates the ill effects of a proud man's looking
when he could have and should have averted his eyes.
Gower's story of Acteon may not be as moving as Ovid's,
but it is more economical, and it serves well the moral
which Gower puts into the mouth of Genius at the very
end:

> Lo now, my Sone, what it is
> A man to caste his yhe amis,
> Which Acteon hath dere aboght;
> Be war forthi and do it noght.
> For ofte, who that hiede toke,
> Betre is to winke than to loke.
>   (I, 379-84)

Gower's changes entitle Genius to interpret the story
in this way to Amans, for Gower recreates Ovid's story
and carefully adapts it to serve his own purposes.

The Tale of Acis and Galatea (CA, II, 97-200)

--Peter G. Beidler

Ovid's story of Polyphemus's interruption of the love of Acis and Galatea (Metamorphoses, XIII, 738-897) is told largely from the point of view of Galatea, the sea nymph daughter of Nereus. Acis is a handsome lad, just sixteen, whose company Galatea seeks constantly; but at the same time the ugly cyclops Polyphemus, whom she loathes, seeks her company and her love. One day, when she is lying in the arms of Acis on the shore, hidden behind a rock, she sees the love-sick Polyphemus on the hillside above them. Not seeing the lovers, he speaks his lament to the waves. Galatea overhears the long and moving speech in which Polyphemus praises Galatea's beauty, laments her rejection of him, lists the wealth and gifts he could offer her, and begs her to come up out of the waves to see him. Just as he completes his lament, Polyphemus spies Galatea in the arms of Acis, becomes enraged, and cries out that this will be her last embrace. Galatea escapes by plunging into the waters, leaving Acis to flee the monster on land. Polyphemus pursues Acis, then tears a huge chunk of rock out of the mountainside and hurls it at the fleeing lover. A tip of the rock strikes Acis, crushes him, and buries him. Galatea then uses her powers to transform the red blood flowing from under the rock into a blue river.

One of Gower's most striking changes in his version of Ovid's story is to make the personages in it far more human. Acis, who in Ovid's account was the son of Faunus (a Pan-like deity) and a sea nymph, becomes for Gower merely a "Bacheler" (II, 125), a "yonge knyht" (II, 131). Galatea, who in Ovid was a sea nymph with

11

special powers, becomes simply a lovely woman. Later,
unlike Ovid's Galatea, who escaped from Polyphemus
simply by diving into the waters (her home), Gower's
human Galatea must be rescued by Neptune, the ruler of
the sea, who is not even mentioned in the Ovid story:

> And as sche fledde fro the londe,
> Neptunus tok hire into honde
> And kept hire in so sauf a place
> Fro Polipheme and his manace.
> (II, 179-82)

Ovid's Galatea did not need supernatural help because
she had supernatural powers herself.

Gower even finds ways to humanize Polyphemus, the
enormous, shaggy, one-eyed cyclops. Gower says nothing
about his being a cyclops, nothing about his having
only a single eye, nothing about his shaggy head,
beard, and body, and almost nothing about his size.
Gower does mention that he is a "Geant" (II, 155), but
that term does not for Gower seem to have suggested
supernatural powers or even extremely abnormal size.
It is interesting to note that whereas Ovid's
Polyphemus broke off, lifted up, and then threw at Acis
an enormous chunk of the mountain, Gower's Polyphemus,
with his far more human limitations of size and
strength, merely shoves part of the bank down and
relies on gravity to convey the death-blow at Acis:

> This Geant with his ruide myht
> Part of the banke he schof doun riht,
> The which evene upon Acis fell.
> (II, 173-75)

Why does Gower want to humanize the three characters
from Ovid's story? Surely the primary reason is that
he wants the lover's predicament in his version of the
story to be as similar as possible to that of Amans,
for if Genius's lessons are to have meaning for his
pupil, then they must derive from situations which are
like the pupil's. The problems of an enormous, hairy,
one-eyed cyclops and his hopeless love for a sea nymph
would scarcely have seemed directly applicable to Amans
and his hopeless love for a human woman.

The applicability of Polyphemus's situation to that
of Amans apparently also has a great deal to do with
certain other changes Gower makes in his version of the
story. For example, Gower changes the sexual love-play
between Galatea and Acis to mere verbal love-play in

his account. Whereas in Ovid's account Polyphemus observed the lovers lying in each other's arms, in Gower's account Polyphemus observes them "in prive place wher thei stode/ To speke and have here wordes goode" (II, 140-42).

This change from love-making to love-talking makes Polyphemus's situation closer to that which Amans himself has already described:

> Whan I the Court se of Cupide
> Aproche unto my ladi side
> Of hem that lusti ben and freisshe,--
> Thogh it availe hem noght a reisshe,
> Bot only that thei ben in speche,--
> My sorwe is thanne noght to seche.
> (II, 39-44)

This change also serves subtly to alter the characterization of the two chief characters, Galatea and Polyphemus, so that they more accurately convey Genius's lesson to Amans.

Gower makes Galatea considerably more attractive than she was in Ovid's version. We have already seen that Gower has her engage only in love-talk with Acis, whereas in Ovid she engaged rather explicitly in sex with him. In addition, Gower's Galatea seems less selfish. To give only one example, in Ovid's story Galatea plunged into the sea to save herself as soon as she saw that Polyphemus was about to attack, leaving her lover, despite his desperate pleas to her for help, to fend for himself. In Gower's version Galatea stays by Acis's side until he is dead, and only then saves herself. Gower made these changes to lay the blame for the misfortune squarely on Polyphemus rather than on Galatea.

In Ovid's account Polyphemus was a rather attractive character, if only because fully half of the story was taken up with his heart-felt lament. Gower omits this lament entirely. Indeed, instead of Galatea's overhearing Polyphemus's words, as happened on Ovid, Gower has Polyphemus remain silent and has him overhear <u>her</u> words to Acis. As a result of this important change, Gower denies us access to Polyphemus's point of view, and so prevents us from sympathizing with him. Then, further to undermine sympathy for Polyphemus, Gower suggests that his crime is a premeditated act, not an impulsive one. In Ovid, Polyphemus murdered Acis in a fit of anger immediately

after he chanced to see him with Galatea; Gower's
Polyphemus, on the other hand, carefully waits and
watches to find the lovers together. Then, after he
does see Acis and Galatea together, he retreats,
roaring like a wild beast. He runs about Mount Aetna,
consumed with sorrow. At length he decides that, even
though he can do himself no good by it, he can at least
bring grief to Acis. He returns to where he earlier
saw the lovers, and kills Acis. This is no impulsive
action inspired by anger, as it was in Ovid; it is an
act of premeditated revenge inspired by jealousy.

   Polyphemus's envy of Acis, of course, is the
central and controlling motive in Gower's story, for
Liber Secundus is about the ill effects of this, the
second of the Seven Deadly Sins. Gower's changes
contribute directly to a strengthening of the emphasis
on envy. Ovid's Polyphemus was apparently jealous of
Acis, but was never explicitly said to be so. Gower's
Polyphemus, unlike Ovid's, is made guilty of the sin of
envy. Five times Gower tells us that Polyphemus feels
"Envie" of Acis (II, 135, 150, 168, 183, 199). He also
tells us that Polyphemus is "Fulfild of sorghe and gret
desese,/ That he syh Acis wel at ese" (II, 165-66).
Surely Gower includes these lines because he uses the
story of Acis and Galatea as a demonstration of the
first of the five kinds of envy: sorrow over another
man's joy. Gower's Polyphemus does sorrow when he sees
Acis happy in love, and his revenge when he sees this
is based entirely on envy.

   Gower shows that he is in full control of his plot
and characterization, for he carefully fits both to his
theme about the ill effects of envy. For his purposes,
Gower needed a pair of human lovers to be the
sympathetic victims of a third lover's envy. And he
needed a plot which focused on the unequivocably sinful
and envious actions of the third lover. Because he did
not find quite the plot or the characters he needed in
Ovid's tale of Acis and Galatea, he exercises his
poet's license and recreates the story. The result is
a pointed lesson for Amans, and for Gower's readers,
about the necessity to avoid envy.

The Tale of Deianira and Nessus (CA, II, 2145-2307)

--Carole Koepke Brown

Ovid's narrative of unjustified pain and sorrow
(IX, 93-133) opens with Hercules and his bride standing
before the swollen river Evenus that blocks their route
home. The centaur Nessus approaches to suggest that he
carry the lovely Deianira across. Although Deianira
fears Nessus as much as she fears the river, Hercules
accepts the plan, and Nessus fords the river with her.
Hercules follows, but, on reaching the bank, he hears
his wife shriek, for Nessus is abducting her. The
unflapable husband delivers a scolding speech and then
shoots the centaur with a poisoned arrow. Nessus
wrenches it out, and, for revenge, gives Deianira his
blood-and-poison-stained garment as a love charm.
Years later, while the dutiful Hercules is fulfilling a
vow in a ritual before the altar of Jupiter, Rumor
tells Deianira that her husband now loves Iole.
Frantically she vacillates among several options, then,
to regain his love, sends her messenger Lichas with
Nessus's lethal robe to Hercules, who puts it on while
performing the sacred ritual. The heat from the sacred
flame on the altar causes the fatal garment to adhere
to his skin. In trying to take off the robe, the
tormented man rips off his own skin. Then the hero, in
an extended plea to his stepmother Juno, questions
justice by enumerating each of his twelve labors and
then contrasts these heroic accomplishments with his
present pathetic condition. In his frenzied agony, he
levels trees on Mt. Aetna. When he spies the innocent
messenger Lichas, Hercules flings him into space, where
he is transformed into a stone that falls into the sea.
The uprooted trees, arranged by the hero into a funeral
pyre, are lighted by Philoctetes, who also receives

15

Hercules' bow and quiver. The hero, now on the funeral
pyre, serenely accepts his own cremation. Meanwhile,
Jupiter confidently announces to his fellow deities
that only the mortal part of his son Hercules (born of
his union with the human Alcmena) will perish. Even
Hercules' petulant stepmother seems to assent. After
Hercules is compared to a glistening snake shedding its
old skin, Jupiter provides a royal chariot to transport
immortal Hercules to the heavens.

Gower not only retains Nessus's two dastardly
deeds--abducting Deianira and giving her a love
charm--in order to dramatize the evils of
"Falssemblant" one of five kinds of envy, but he also
moves them to center stage in order to intensify his
didactic purpose. As Genius explains before he relates
the tale:

> For Falssemblant hath everemo
> Of his conseil in compaignie
> The derke untrewe Ypocrisie,
> Whos word descordeth to his thoght.
> (II, 1890-93)

We can see how Gower alters the Ovidian story by his
handling of the three major characters.

First, whereas Ovid was interested in Deianira as a
character in her own right, Gower is more interested in
her as an innocent victim of another's hypocrisy. Ovid
took us into her mind when she feared Nessus before
they crossed the river, and, in a psychologically
perceptive monologue, when she distractedly cast about
among various alternatives for a means to regain her
husband's love. Ovid told no more of her after she
sent the lethal garment to Hercules, although the
narrative continued for more than one hundred lines.
Gower, on the other hand, stresses her status as a
victim. He omits her initial fears and her monologue,
but adds Nessus's explanation of the potency of the
love charm and her trusting acceptance of his present.
Gower also depicts her joy:

> Who was tho glad bot Deianyre?
> Hire thoghte hire herte was afyre
> Til it was in hire cofre loke,
> So that no word therof was spoke.
> (II, 2255-58)

16

These additions of her good faith and joy set her up as the victim of Nessus's machinations. Gower also emphasizes the effects of Nessus's hypocrisy when, years later, she recalls his instructions as she gives the lethal garment to her husband: "To such entente as she was bede/ Of Nessus" (II, 2284-85). Moreover, although Ovid dropped her after approximately one-third of the story, Gower refers to her remorse again at the end of the story by observing that she is "sori for everemo" (II, 2307). Gower is less interested in her as a unique individual than Ovid was, and telescopes her role to make her both subordinate to Nessus and a reminder of his hypocrisy.

And whereas Ovid focused his story on Hercules, Gower gives Hercules a much smaller role and makes him dramatically less heroic. Consider some of Gower's more significant omissions: Hercules' threatening speech immediately before shooting Nessus; Hercules' ritual before the altar of Jupiter; Hercules' extended plea to Juno questioning the management of the universe; Hercules' punishment of Lichas. While Gower keeps the general outline of Ovid's story, he mutes the gristly physical specifics. For example, Gower gives a sketchy review of how Hercules' shirt clings to his body, but omits the fire eating up the hero's intestines, the sweat flowing, the sinews cracking, and the bones dissolving. Gower chooses not to describe the physical horror of a burn victim but rather chooses, again, to stress the moral horror of hypocrisy.

Gower also wants a more human Hercules, one closer to Amans. As the story opened, Ovid characterized his brawny, calm hero by showing Hercules' contempt for the easy way across the river. Strikingly different is Gower's Hercules, who knows "noght the forde ariht" (II, 2166) and even seeks counsel from Nessus:

> And axen him if that he wiste
> What thing hem were best to done,
> So that thei mihten sauf and sone
> The water passe, he and sche.
> (II, 2186-89)

More evidence showing how Gower makes his Hercules flawed is Hercules' behavior with his new lover, Iole. His acquiescence to Iole's suggestion that they wear each other's clothes indicates a weakness of character not found in his Ovidian counterpart:

17

And sche made Hercules so nyce
Upon hir Love and so assote,
That he him clotheth in hire cote,
And sche in his was clothed ofte;
And thus fieblesce is set alofte,
And strengthe was put under fote,
Ther can noman therof do bote.
                    (II, 2268-74)

As Macaulay notes (Vol. 1, p. 489), Gower could have
drawn from Ovid's Deianira Herculi (in the Herodites)
the incident in which Hercules and a new lover wore
each other's clothes. Even if Gower drew from this
second Ovidian source, however, in doing so he
consciously weakens and humanizes Hercules. In
addition, of course, he foreshadows Hercules' wearing
of the garment poisoned by Nessus.

     Gower also omits Ovid's final, dramatic event:
Hercules' apotheosis. Gower omits Jupiter's rhetorical
announcement to the gods about his son's deification,
the reaction from Juno, the simile of the snake
shedding its skin, and the chariot trip to the stars.
Though Hercules was venerable at the end of Ovid's
story, Gower's final comment shows his human
vulnerability. The sound of his burning "fleissh and
bones" (II, 2302) resounds in the final lines. Gower
has no interest in having his readers contemplate
heavenly justice or celebrate a hero. Rather, he wants
to keep attention firmly on Nessus and the evils of
hypocrisy. Accordingly, he reduces Hercules' role and
heightens Nessus's villainy in both hypocritical acts.

     In the first, Gower takes us into Nessus's
consciousness. Ovid's Nessus simply approached the
stranded newlyweds and, with seeming virtuousness,
suggested, "I'll carry her. You swim." Gower,
however, dramatizes Nessus's resolve by taking us into
Nessus's mind even before his first word to Hercules
and Deianira. And Gower fittingly attributes the
villainy to Envy, the dominant vice for Liber Secundus:

          Withinne his herte he gan conspire,
          As he which thurgh his tricherie
          Hath Hercules in gret envie,
          Which he bar in his herte loke,
          And thanne he thoghte it schal be wroke.
                         (II, 2170-74)

Gower increases Nessus's villainy because the abduction
is clearly premeditated. This villainy is reinforced

when Nessus arrives on the far side of the river and
knowingly confirms his resolve to "sette his trowthe al
out of mynde" (II, 2226). Gower allows Nessus's mental
process to incriminate him.

In Nessus's second hypocritical act, where Ovid
pictured Nessus promising himself revenge before he
handed over his garment, Genius expands Nessus's
instructions to Deianira to keep it "prively" (II,
2247), and looks into the future: should the love of
"hire lord" (II, 2248) stray, the robe has power to
return his love to her. Gower could have consulted the
brief story in Mythographi Vaticani (I, 58) and noted
the dramatization of Nessus's instructions, but
although there Nessus explains the love charm more
thoroughly than he had in Ovid, still Nessus does not
counsel secrecy. Perhaps Gower adds the secrecy to
stress what Genius explains before he tells the story:

> Wher that Envie thenkth to guile,
> He schal be for that ilke while
> Of prive conseil Messagier.
> (II, 1915-17)

Gower elects to throw emphasis on Nessus's counsel to
Deianira in order to demonstrate more clearly for Amans
that Nessus's deceitful words are part of a revenge
plot. And, while Ovid omitted both Deianira and Nessus
in the last two-thirds of the tale, Gower chooses to
focus on "the false wiht" (II, 2240) as he concludes
his admonition:

> Which thing cam al thurgh Falssemblant,
> That false Nessus the Geant
> Made unto him and to his wif;
> Wherof that he hath lost his lif,
> And sche sori for everemo.
> (II, 2303-07)

In brief, then, although Gower retains some of the
basic events in Ovid's story, he makes Deianira more
clearly the victim, makes Hercules less significant and
less heroic, and makes Nessus more significant and more
heinous. These transformations serve to admonish Amans
to "let thi Semblant be trewe and plein" (II, 1912).
Although both Ovid's and Gower's tales concern
unjustified pain and sorrow, Gower's concentrates not
on the effect for Hercules, but on Nessus's envious
hypocrisy.

19

The Tale of Pyramus and Thisbe (CA, III, 1331-1494)

--Judith C. G. Moran

As Ovid tells it, the story of Pyramus and Thisbe
(Metamorphoses, IV, 55-166) is a story of tragically
thwarted love. Although the lovers are kept apart
physically by a wall separating their homes and by
their parents, who forbid them to meet, nothing can
constrain their love, which increases daily. When they
discover a crack in the wall through which they whisper
of their love each day, they make plans to meet
secretly one night outside the city. When the time
comes they arrive at their rendezvous separately.
Thisbe arrives first, is frightened by a lioness, and
drops her veil as she flees to a nearby cave. The
lioness finds the veil and shreds it with teeth and
claws bloodied by a recent kill. When Pyramus arrives,
he sees the paw prints and the bloody veil and assumes
that Thisbe is dead. Blaming himself for her death, he
carries her veil to the place where they were to have
met--in the shade of the mulberry tree near Ninus's
tomb. In his anguish he plunges his sword into his
side. His blood soaks the ground and stains the fruit
and berries of the tree dark purple. Soon Thisbe
returns to find Pyramus near death. After fleeting
recognition, he dies in her arms. Blaming herself and
unwilling to let death separate them, Thisbe kills
herself as well. Both the gods and the parents have
pity on the dead lovers; the fruit of the mulberry tree
to this day remains purple in memory of their deaths,
and the ashes of the lovers are joined forever in a
single urn.

Both Chaucer and Gower write versions of the story
based on Ovid's tale. G. C. Macaulay feels that

21

Gower's is the inferior rendition:

> When we compare the results, we find that in this
> instance it is Chaucer who has followed his
> authority closely, while Gower gives a paraphrase
> in his own language and with several variations of
> detail. He says, for example, that the lovers
> themselves made the hole in the wall through which
> they conversed; he omits Ninus' tomb; he speaks of
> a lion, not a lioness; he says that Thisbe hid
> herself in a bush (not a cave), and that then the
> lion slew and devoured a beast before drinking at
> the spring; he cuts short the speech of Pyramus
> before killing himself; he represents that Pyramus
> was slain at once instead of living until Thisbe
> came; he invents an entirely new speech for Thisbe;
> and he judiciously omits, as Chaucer does also, the
> mention of the mulberry tree and its
> transformation.
>
> In short, Gower writes apparently from a general
> recollection of the story, while Chaucer evidently
> has his Ovid before him and endeavors to translate
> almost every phrase, showing thereby his good
> taste, for Ovid tells the story well. (Macaulay,
> English Works, volume 1, pp. 497-98.)

Macaulay, however, surely overlooks the purpose and
effect of Gower's changes. Far from having an inferior
recollection of the story, Gower adapts it to serve
quite different needs.

All of Ovid's tales were concerned with
metamorphoses, and his avowed purpose for telling the
story of Pyramus and Thisbe was to explain why the
once-white fruit and berries of the mulberry tree are
purple. The lovers' tragedy provides the reason. It
is a forthrightly sentimental tale told for its
emotional appeal among a group of young girls. To
heighten this appeal, Ovid punctuated it with several
emotional apostrophes by the ill-fated lovers, and
placed emphasis on the visual contrast of the snow-
white fruit and the deep purple of the lovers' blood.
Gower, no doubt, found much to admire in Ovid's highly
emotional tale, but adapted it to his own didactic
purpose. Liber Tercius is concerned with an exposition
of the servants of Wrath, one of which is foolhaste.
Pyramus's suicide, based on purely circumstantial
evidence, must have seemed a perfect example of
foolhaste, for even a small amount of patience (the
cure of all Wrath) surely would have spared both

Pyramus's life and Thisbe's. Gower's focus in adaptation, then, is on the plot elements that reinforce the conclusion that Pyramus, in killing himself, acts hastily, foolishly, and impatiently.

Gower first eliminates the mulberry tree as the generative force of the story, then pares out sentimental detail to make way for his lesson. He retains the isolating wall motif, but, significantly, omits all mention of the parents. The wall is now the only impediment to the happiness of the lovers.

Gower also makes his lovers more active in their efforts to be together and thus quickens the pace of the story. They do not simply find a crack in the wall; they themselves create a hole (III, 1370-71) and plan explicitly the arrangements of their secret meeting (III, 1376-83). While Ovid's lovers went daily to the wall to whisper and lament their separation, Gower makes it clear that they make the hole in one day and plan to meet the same night--an example of foolhaste. A less impatient pair might have formulated plans less apt to go awry.

Gower's Pyramus and Thisbe, like Ovid's, agree to meet beneath a tree, but the tree has no significance beyond marking the meeting place. Ovid placed his tree in a secluded graveyard, but in Gower it stands next to a more public well, where the lovers are more likely to be seen--further indication of hasty planning if they are truly concerned with secrecy. When Thisbe arrives at the tree, she is frightened by a lion. In Ovid the lioness was bloody from a kill it had just made. It was ferocious looking and frightened Thisbe, but it was presumably not still hungry. Gower's lion, on the other hand, comes "into the feld to take his preie" (III, 1393). He is not bloody yet but, for that reason, presents a more clear and present danger from which Thisbe must flee. Thisbe runs, dropping her wimple, and takes shelter beneath a bush, less secluded than Ovid's cave but still secure. The lion then kills an animal, drinks from the spring, and, as in Ovid, tears and bloodies the wimple which Pyramus finds when he arrives moments later.

In using the unnecessary death of Pyramus as an example of the effects of foolhaste, Gower reduces both description and speech to the barest minimum. And, as before, he reduces the time in which a decision is made. When Pyramus finds Thisbe's wimple, his heart is

stricken and he wrings his hands, thinking surely she
is dead:

> and sodeinly
> His swerd al nakid out he breide
> In his folhaste, and thus he seide:
> "I am cause of this felonie,
> So it is resoun that I die,
> As sche is ded be cause of me."
> (III, 1428-33)

Then he cries up to heaven itself:

> And preide, sithen it was so
> That he may noght his love as tho
> Have in this world, that of her grace
> He miht hire have in other place,
> For hiere wolde he noght abide.
> (III, 1437-41)

With that he falls forward on his sword, which pierces
his heart. His action is swift and completely self-
centered. By abandoning himself fully to grief and
foolhaste, Pyramus seals Thisbe's fate as well as his
own.

Gower has indeed made the changes in Ovid's story
that Macaulay took note of--but for very good reasons.
Liber Tercius has as its overall message the idea that
love is good and natural and should not be hindered in
its fulfillment. Patience and avoidance of Wrath in
all its forms (especially foolhaste) are necessary if
lovers are to keep themselves from becoming their own
hindrance to fulfillment. Pyramus fails on both
counts, says Gower, and tragically forfeits not one
life but two.

24

The Tale of Phebus and Daphne (CA, III, 1685-1720)

--Natalie Epinger Ruyak

Ovid tells the story of Phebus and Daphne (Metamorphoses, I, 452-567) in order to elicit sympathy from the reader for the virgin nymph, Daphne. One day, Phebus makes the mistake of insulting Cupid for toying with arrows which could kill neither animals nor humans. Out of spite, Cupid puts two of his arrows to devious use: he shoots a golden arrow into Phebus and a lead arrow into Daphne. This causes Phebus to fall passionately in love with the beautiful Daphne. Daphne, however, because of the lead arrow, shuns the very idea of love, and prefers to roam the woodlands, emulating the goddess Diana. The lovesick Phebus tries to woo Daphne. Frightened, she tries to run away from him, but Phebus is swifter and eventually catches up. Arriving at the river Peneus, Daphne, weary from flight, cries for help from her father, the god of the river, begging for some sort of transformation. Peneus responds to her plea. Suddenly Daphne's body becomes enclosed by bark. Her hair grows into foliage, her arms become branches, her feet become roots, and her face becomes the treetop. Phebus's passion is so great that he still loves Daphne even though she is now a tree, and he tells her that she will bear the laurel for athletes' crowns and will stand as guardian by Augustus's gateposts. The tree nods in the wind as though assenting.

Ovid's descriptive and moving account is greatly simplified in the Confessio Amantis. Gower drastically reduces the story by omitting the nature imagery, the long description of Phebus's chase, Daphne's prayers begging for a transformation, the detailed account of

25

the transformation, and Phebus's speech to the laurel
tree. Gower reduces the plot from over a hundred lines
in Ovid to a mere thirty-five lines, and then spends
another twenty-five lines explaining the moral of the
story. This reveals Gower's intention in telling the
story: not to entertain, but to teach a lesson about
the dangers of foolhaste. Gower warns that love cannot
be attained by impetuous behavior. It is fitting,
therefore, that Gower's version, unlike Ovid's, shows
Phebus to be smitten with foolhaste before Cupid's
arrow pierces him. Thus, Cupid is changed from the
creator of passions in Ovid's story to the mere
intensifier of already existing emotions in Gower's
version. Appropriately, Gower begins his tale by
drawing attention immediately to Phebus's passion and
foolhaste on the one hand and to Daphne's aversion to
love on the other:

> Phebus his love hath on hire leid,
> And therupon to hire he soghte
> In his folhaste, and so besoghte,
> That sche with him no reste hadde;
> For evere upon hire love he gradde,
> And sche seide evere unto him nay.
>   (III, 1688-93)

Cupid's arrows, therefore, merely heighten the emotions
of the characters, and Gower is able to omit all of the
description related to the arrows themselves. Instead
of stating explicitly why Cupid shoots the two with the
arrows, Gower briefly alludes to the incident, implying
that Cupid's act is an attempt to teach the hasty
Phebus a lesson by making him even more foolhasty:

> Cupide, which hath every chance
> Of love under his governance,
> Syh Phebus hasten him so sore:
> And for he scholde him haste more,
> And yit noght speden ate laste,
> A dart thurghout his herte he caste.
>   (III, 1695-1700)

A significant difference between the two works is
that Ovid's tale revealed greater sympathy for Daphne
than Gower's does. This is due partly to Gower's
narrative point of view; whereas Ovid recorded Daphne's
thoughts, Gower never reveals them. Gower purposefully
heads off any feelings of sympathy the reader might
have for Daphne since these would detract from the
moral focus on Phebus's foolhaste. Ovid created more
interest in his characters by showing them conversing.

26

Gower, however, tells his version of the tale as an exemplum, a story about how not to act with foolhaste. Only after Gower relates the tale does he resort to dialogue, and then only to let Genius point out to Amans the dangers of foolhaste and impatience. Another way Gower detracts from sympathy for Daphne is by making her rejection of Phebus a personal one. Unlike Ovid, Gower does not suggest that she wants to protect her virginity and is thus rejecting all men; instead, she seems to be denying Phebus simply because she does not like <u>Phebus</u>. Gower eliminates Daphne's desire to remain a virgin, because, once again, it would detract from his main focus on foolhaste. It is not important for Gower to tell us whether or not Daphne was trying to keep her virginity, but it is important for Gower to point out the foolish haste with which Phebus falls in love and his impatience in attempting to win over his maiden.

Also significant is that Gower makes his story more realistic than Ovid's by making Daphne a maiden instead of a nymph, and by making her more accessible to Phebus than Ovid had. Gower makes the lovers more human, and so more like Amans. Thus, Amans can more easily relate Phebus's problem of foolhaste to his own, and he can more easily apply the lesson to his own situation.

Gower successfully transforms Ovid's story into an original creation. He maintains Ovid's basic plot, but eliminates all of the extraneous details which would overshadow his warning against foothaste.

The Tale of Pygmalion (CA, IV, 371-436)

--Carole Koepke Brown

The account of Pygmalion in Ovid's Metamorphoses
(X, 243-97) celebrates the power of man's creativity
and piety. Pygmalion, a highly gifted sculptor, long
elects bachelorhood because he is offended by the
morally reprehensible women called Propoetides and,
more generally, by woman's evil nature. After he
sculpts a life-like ivory virgin, he is smitten with
love for it. He treats the statue as if it were alive,
for he touches it and puts it into bed. Then, when the
festival of Venus arrives, the genuinely pious
Pygmalion attends. He timidly asks the Goddess of Love
that his wife be like his ivory maiden. After the
omens prove favorable, Venus grants his unspoken
prayer: that his statue come to life. Having quickly
returned home, Pygmalion kisses and touches the statue.
The ivory warms and softens. Pygmalion rejoices that
it is coming to life, yet simultaneously fears that he
is deceived. But he feels her veins throb, and he is
thankful. He mentally formulates extravagant
expressions of gratitude for Venus. The ivory maiden,
as she begins to feel his kisses, blushes and opens her
eyes. They wed and, nine months later, have a son,
Paphos. Art has brought the recluse Pygmalion back
into human community.

Gower retains Ovid's basic narrative thread: an
artist makes a beautiful ivory figure, falls in love
with it, woos it, asks Venus to bring it to life, and
rejoices as it comes alive. Then he weds his lovely
maiden and, with her, engenders an heir. Yet the
stories are far from identical. Gower de-emphasizes
Venus and the ivory maiden, lowers Pygmalion's age,

29

humanizes him, and--most important for Gower's moral
purpose--makes his taciturn Ovidian counterpart into an
aggressively verbal Pygmalion. By reshaping the
material in the Metamorphoses, Gower dramatically
alters the narrative to illustrate a specific moral not
in his source. Genius states this moral after Amans
confesses that he "dar noght speke" to his "ladi" (IV,
360, 362). Genius advises the lover continually to
pray and beseech:

> Mi Sone, do nomore so:
> For after that a man poursuieth
> To love, so fortune suieth,
> Fulofte and yifth hire happi chance
> To him which makth continuance
> To preie love and to beseche;
> As be ensample I schal thee teche.
>   (IV, 364-70)

In other words, Genius is exhorting Amans to avoid a
particular kind of Sloth, pusillanimity, which the
opening section defines as lacking "bothe word and
dede,/ Wherof he scholde his cause spede" (IV, 323-24),
but Genius's admonition and story focus only on the
lack of word.

     To make this point clearly, Gower writes virtually
a one-character tale. Venus receives almost no
attention. Ovid set up elaborate preparations for the
feast in honor of Venus even before she heard
Pygmalion's request, then depicted the goddess
compassionately intuiting the intent of Pygmalion's
halting prayer to let his wife be like his statue. In
the Confessio Amantis, on the other hand, the goddess
speaks only one line, that one merely announcing that
she grants his request. There are no white-necked
heifers being slaughtered, no frankincense, no omens,
and no festival. Moreover, Pygmalion's wife in Ovid's
story was a modest, timid, and blushing virgin, for
Ovid was contrasting her with the brash Propoetides.
Gower omits her modesty, her blushing, and her bashful
looks. At the end of the story she is called merely
"lusti" and "obeissant" (IV, 424, 425). Yet,
significantly, Gower adds to his source a description
of the statue's speech-producing features: "Sche was
rody on the cheke/ And red on bothe hire lippes eke"
(IV, 385-86). This description helps prepare the
reader to focus on Pygmalion's speaking. By
de-emphasizing the two minor characters--Venus and the
wife--in his source, Gower centers our sympathies more
exclusively on Pygmalion.

To drive home Genius's instructions to Amans, Gower retains Pygmalion's love-stricken condition, for Amans can easily identify with that, and makes Pygmalion "a lusti man of yowthe" (IV, 373), whereas Ovid suggested that he had lived single for a long time.

Similarly, Gower humanizes the sculptor. Ovid implicitly suggested that Pygmalion was almost deific. As the ivory was coming to life under Pygmalion's tender fingertips, Ovid offered a simile of wax being softened by the sun, the sun representing Pygmalion. Similarly, when the ivory maiden became animated and first opened her eyes, she saw her lover and the heavens at the same moment. In these two instances, Ovid implied a natural association between Pygmalion and the suprahuman. Gower gives his Pygmalion more human proportions. Whereas Ovid, on one level, explored what _art_ could work, Gower develops what the persistent _word_ might accomplish. And Gower wants to praise the efficacy of words spoken by a character somewhat more human than Ovid's Pygmalion. Gower's sculptor may be gifted "above alle othre men" (IV, 375), yet he is less divine than Ovid's. Gower does not associate anything extraterrestrial with his Pygmalion. Instead, Gower wants his Pygmalion to be close to the earth so that the penitent Amans can more readily identify with him.

Even more telling than making Pygmalion somewhat more human is the dramatic change Gower fashions in Pygmalion's verbal ability. In Ovid's rendering, Pygmalion was reticent, but this was _not_ treated as a character defect. Ovid explained that Pygmalion would pray timidly, then interrupted Pygmalion's direct discourse to say that Pygmalion did not dare to ask explicitly that his sculpture be brought to life. That he did not plead more verbosely was not detrimental to his cause. Indeed, it increased his piety, for it suggested genuine deference to Venus. And, in response to Venus's gift, Ovid's Pygmalion merely thought, but did not articulate, his gratitude.

Very different is the verbal expression of Gower's Pygmalion. Within the frame of Gower's adaptation, avoiding speech is sin:

> Forthi, my Sone, if that thou spare
> To speke, lost is al thi fare,
> For Slowthe bringth in alle wo.
> (IV, 439-41)

Both Ovid's and Gower's lovesick Pygmalions speak
frequently to their ivory figures, but Gower not only
retains the three instances from Ovid, but also adds
one more (IV, 393, 398, 407, 410). And whereas Ovid's
bashful Pygmalion only hinted at his true desire,
Gower's Pygmalion is a human prayer wheel. Gower could
have gotten the idea for Pygmalion's extended prayer
from Jean de Meun's account of Pygmalion in Roman de la
Rose, where his prayer runs twenty-five lines, yet de
Meun's Venus accepts the prayer because Pygmalion
renounces chastity. In the Confessio Amantis, however,
it is the duration of the prayer that moves Venus to
accomplish the miracle:

> Bot how it were, of his penance
> He made such continuance
> Fro dai to nyht, and preith so longe,
> That his preiere is underfonge,
> Which Venus of hire grace herde.
>   (IV, 415-19)

Significantly, this is cast as a Latinate clause: the
prayer had such length that, as a result, Venus accepts
the plea. Although Ovid's Venus granted the
petitioner's request in part because of his not daring
to verbalize it entirely, Gower's Venus grants it only
because the petitioner "dorste speke" (IV, 429). Then,
for emphasis, Gower outlines a scenario in the
subjunctive which is not in his source: "And if he
wolde have holde him stille/ And nothing spoke, he
scholde have failed" (IV, 426-27).

While Gower, then, retains Ovid's narrative thread,
he shapes the story to feature a new moral. So that
the instruction will be more appropriate to Amans,
Gower humanizes Pygmalion. So that the evils of
pusillanimity are utterly clear, Gower de-emphasizes
Venus and the wife and gives his Pygmalion verbal
tenacity. And so that Genius's point that "word mai
worche above kinde" (IV, 438) may be clear, Gower has
Venus respond only after Pygmalion's request has been
both long and full.

The Tale of Iphis (CA, IV, 451-505)

--Nicolette Stasko

Ovid's story about Iphis (Metamorphorses, IX, 666-797) tells of a poor but free-born man named Ligdus. Ligdus is forced by his poverty to make a harsh decision regarding the birth of his forthcoming child. He tells his wife, Telethusa, that if it is a female child it must be killed. Shortly before the child is born, however, the goddess Isis appears in a dream to Telethusa and tells her that she should let the child live regardless of its sex. When the child is born a female, Telethusa, heeding the advice of the goddess, orders it to be reared as a male to fool Ligdus. When Iphis reaches the age of thirteen, Ligdus arranges for Iphis to marry Ianthe, a girl of the same age. The two fall in love, but Iphis, who knows the truth of the situation, despairs of ever finding happiness with Ianthe. After postponing the marriage with various excuses, Telethusa makes a touching plea to the goddess Isis, who takes pity and transforms Iphis into a young man. The long-awaited wedding uniting the joyful lovers then takes place.

Gower changes the story considerably. He maintains the basic story line but, by changing a few details, completely shifts the emphasis of the tale and alters its meaning to fit his own purpose, which is to show how a "busy" and persevering heart protects lovers from falling into the sin of sloth.

The first of Gower's changes is to make Ligdus a king rather than a poor commoner. This change not only brings the tale closer to the situation of Amans, who is a courtly knight, but also makes Ligdus seem more cruel and unreasonable. In Ovid's version Ligdus was somewhat justified in sorrowfully refusing to raise a female child because of his extreme poverty. In Gower's version, however, the king has no motivation beyond a vague "strif" (IV, 451) for ordering a daughter to be put to death. In making this change, Gower is perhaps emphasizing the dangers of irresponsible kingship, and also eliciting increased sympathy for the distraught Telethusa and her unfortunate daughter, the victims of a cruel and unnecessary fate.

Another change Gower makes is to reduce greatly the importance of the goddess Isis. She becomes merely the goddess of "childinge" (IV, 461) and has influence only over the events of the story relating directly to the birth and preservation of the new-born Iphis. In Gower's version she has no part in the transformation of Iphis into a young man, as she had in Ovid's. Instead, to fit the tale to his theme of the wonders wrought by steadfast love, Gower introduces the figure of Cupid, the symbol of love, who then takes pity on Iphis and transforms her.

A third change Gower makes is to eliminate Iphis's lengthy speech in which she despairs of ever consummating her unnatural love for Ianthe. Gower omits this speech for two reasons. First, because this tale occurs in the section on sloth dealing with pusillanimity, Gower wants to show that Iphis is not afraid to begin an action--in this case a marriage action. She neither makes excuses for her love nor complains about her unfortunate circumstances, as Ovid's Iphis had done. Second, Gower prefers not to emphasize the unnaturalness of the love by calling special attention to it in the speech.

A fourth change is closely related to this last one, for Gower similarly avoids making the love of Iphis and Ianthe a sexually unnatural one by lowering the ages of the lovers from thirteen (the age of puberty) to ten, a more innocent age. Another advantage of Gower's reduction of the age of marriage is that the two children can then spend several years innocently tumbling in bed like playmates: "Togedre as thei ben pleiefieres/ Liggende abedde upon a nyht" (IV, 482-83). This lengthening of time between marriage and consummation is particularly suited to Gower's purpose since he wishes to show how a busy heart and a love which is ever persistent without sloth will be rewarded. Because the two girls endure their

34

"unnatural" love for so long without complaint, Cupid, the messenger of love, takes pity on them and transforms Iphis into a young man so that a natural union may take place: "Wherof Cupide thilke throwe/ Tok pite for the grete love" (IV, 488-89). Gower re-emphasizes his theme at the end of the tale when he has Genius state:

> It semeth love is welwillende
> To hem that ben continuende
> With besy herte to poursuie
> Thing which that is to love due.
>   (IV, 507-10)

Persistent in his theme and purpose, Gower transforms Ovid's tale about the rewards of prayer and obedience into one about the wonders wrought by enduring and uncomplaining love.

The Tale of Icarus (CA, IV, 1035-71)

--Karl A. Zipf, Jr.

The story of Icarus, as told by Ovid (_Metamorphoses_, VIII, 183-235), is about man's first flight. Daedalus, creator of the Labyrinth and father of Icarus, is forbidden to leave Crete and return to his native Greece. Because King Minos controls both land and sea but not the air, Daedalus decides that flight is the only means of escape. The wings he creates are marvelously built of feathers fastened together by wax. When the wings are finished, Daedalus tries them out and then prepares his son for flight. He warns the boy of the dangers of flying too close to the water and of flying too close to the sun. He advises Icarus to follow him closely. The two make their aerial escape, but when they are over the sea, youthful exuberance takes hold of Icarus. When he flies to great heights, his nearness to the sun causes the wax to melt. Having lost his feathers, Icarus plunges into the water. When Daedalus sees the feathers on the water, he curses his skill. He buries his son, and as he does so a bird appears.

Gower pares away many parts of the plot of this classic tale. He removes all references to Daedalus's greatness and skips the detailed account of the construction of the wings. He mentions neither the island setting nor the ocean. He eliminates the account of Daedalus's grief for the death of his son and of the transformation of Icarus into a bird.

There is a purpose behind Gower's extensive reworking of Ovid's story, for Gower's objectives are different. He is writing about Icarus and the boy's

37

negligence, not about Daedalus and his skill and grief.
In order to make this alteration, Gower reduces the
importance of Daedalus by changing him from a fabulous
inventor to merely a skilled craftsman: "This Dedalus,
which fro his yowthe/ Was tawht and manye craftes
cowthe" (IV, 1047-48).

Although Icarus is the central character in Gower's
tale, Gower develops only one of the boy's
characteristics, his negligence. Liber Quartus
concerns itself with the nature of the sin of sloth,
one type of which is negligence. Gower is concerned
especially with negligence about obeying authority, and
negligence about staying in one's social class. He
states one aspect of his theme in the three
transitional lines between the immediately preceding
tale of Phaeton and the tale of Icarus:

> In hih astat it is a vice
> To go to lowe, and in service
> It grieveth forto go to hye.
> (IV, 1035-37)

The first story in Liber Quartus concerns a boy of
noble birth named Phaeton who flies too low and drowns.
The second story is of Icarus, a boy of lowly birth,
the son of a craftsman, who flies too high and
perishes. In both cases, if the boys had obeyed their
fathers and maintained their designated paths, they
would not have been ruined in their first experiences
at flight.

Evidently, then, Gower uses Icarus to illustrate
his point about social climbing. In Ovid Icarus was
warned about flying too high and too low, but in Gower
the boy is warned only about flying too high, for
Gower's theme is that one should not step above one's
social class. Since Icarus is of lowly birth, it would
be inappropriate to warn him about the dangers of
flying too low, for in flying low he would be in his
natural station, and would be quite safe. This also is
why Gower changes the island setting to a prison
setting and omits all references to water, for Gower
conveniently eliminates the hazards of flying too low
and having the wings grow heavy from the water. Thus,
since there is no reason left for Icarus not to fly
close to the earth, he is quite logically warned only
about the dangers of flying too high. When he does not
heed his father's advice, he dies. Here Gower ends the
story, for to add the details of Daedalus's grief and
of Icarus's transformation into a bird would detract

from the point.

Gower's purpose is to show the consequences of negligence and of aspiring to something beyond one's station in life. Having shown that, he concludes his story with a concise statement of his moral:

> Ther fallen ofte times fele
> For lacke of governance in wele,
> Als wel in love as other weie.
>   (IV, 1069-71)

Knowing full well what he wanted to say, Gower selected the story of Icarus to illustrate his point, and then reworked the version he found in Ovid to make clear his point about the dangers of attempting to rise above one's station.

The Tale of Ceyx and Alceone (CA, IV, 2927-3123)

--John B. Gaston

Ovid's story of the lovers Ceyx and Alceone
(Metamorphoses, IX, 410-748) is a lyrical account of
two people whose love for one another transcends even
death. Ceyx, a king of Trachis, contemplates a voyage
to Claros to consult the oracle there. Alceone, his
wife, begs him not to go or, if he must go, at least to
take her with him. After promising to return within
two months, he sets sail. Midway across the sea, the
ship is engulfed in a violent storm and is slowly
battered to pieces. The captain's orders cannot be
heard in the din. Each man struggles desperately to
save the ship, but it is swamped, and all aboard drown.
By holding on to a piece of wreckage, Ceyx manages to
stay afloat long enough to pray that his body will be
washed up where Alceone will find and bury it.
Alceone, meanwhile, dutifully prays to Juno for her
husband's safe return. Juno, in order to put an end to
her useless pleadings, sends Iris to the home of Sleep
and bids her have that deity send a dream to tell
Alceone of her husband's death. Sleep sends Morpheus
to Alceone, who appears in the form of Ceyx and
describes his death to her. Awakening suddenly,
Alceone mourns inconsolably. In the morning she goes
to the shore, to the spot from which Ceyx set sail, and
relives the parting in her mind. She sees a speck on
the horizon. It drifts slowly toward her until she
recognizes it as the body of Ceyx. Stricken with
grief, she flings herself into the sea. She is
transformed into a bird and attempts to embrace the
corpse with her wings. The gods have pity on her and
restore Ceyx to life as a bird also.

Gower greatly abbreviates the story, yet deletes
almost nothing completely. Most notably, the shipwreck
scene, one hundred lines long in Ovid, is cut to two
lines in Gower: "The tempeste of the blake cloude,/
The wode See, the wyndes loude" (IV, 3063-64). Rather
than forming part of the narrative, the storm is merely
a detail in Alceone's dream. Most of the leavetaking
is deleted, as is Ceyx's pathetic speech in the dream.
Alceone's mourning is much shortened. Surprisingly,
the description of the house of Sleep, which seems at
first reading merely ornamental, is repeated in detail
by Gower.

The effects of the majority of the deletions are
vastly to reduce the role of Ceyx and to concentrate
primarily on Alceone and her dream. The theme of
Gower's story becomes the prophetic power which the
dream displays. In Ovid, Alceone prayed for her
husband's safety, but in Gower she prays for
information. This is appropriate, as the dream then
becomes not a gratuitous revelation, but one dealing
specifically with the information Alceone had
requested. Details of the storm and the activities of
Ceyx become relatively unimportant, while the mechanics
of the dream and its begetting assume greater
significance.

The detailed description of the house of Sleep is
preserved by Gower because it provides a physical
reality for the source of prophetic dreams, and because
it makes palpable an essentially illusory phenomenon.
The dream itself becomes more realistic in that Gower
adds the characters Ithecus and Panthasas, who
dramatize the shipwreck, presenting it vividly both to
Alceone and to the reader. The shift in position of
the wreck scene from the beginning of the story to near
the end (in the dream) provides an element of suspense
lacking in Ovid; the reader is not sure how true the
dream is until Alceone actually finds the body. The
body itself, which in Ovid drifted in as Alceone stood
and watched, is in Gower found on the shore in the very
position it occupies in the dream. Another detail
added by Gower is the skepticism of Alceone's maids,
who, against all logic, insist that the dream "is a
tokne of goode" (IV, 3075). This suggests either that
they really have no faith in the dream or that they are
merely attempting to comfort their distraught mistress.
The finding of the body serves to silence those
skeptical of the prophetic powers of dreams.

Finally, Gower builds sympathy for his heroine by altering her character. Ovid's Alceone was an importunate woman who nagged her husband to take her with him, and who prayed incessantly to Juno to permit her husband's safe return. Gower's Alceone accompanies Ceyx to the shore "forto don him felaschipe" (IV, 2950), and whereas in Ovid Juno sent the dream merely to show Alceone the futility of further prayer, in Gower it is a reward for dutifulness. In the transformation scene, Ovid had Alceone as a bird attempt to embrace Ceyx's corpse. In Gower, the transformation of Ceyx is simultaneous with that of Alceone, so that Alceone greets a live bird in the water, rather than a rotting corpse. In this way, the transformation is seen as a reward to "Alceoun the trewe queene" (IV, 3121), and eliminates an unnecessary pathetic element in the story.

Gower's version loses much of the poetic quality that characterized Ovid's, but it better serves his purpose. Because Gower's story is about the prophetic qualities of dream visions, it focuses on the recipient of the vision and on the mechanism by which the dream vision is bestowed upon her. All unnecessary detail has been carefully eliminated. What remains is almost pure parable, perfectly suited to Gower's purpose.

The Tale of Argus and Mercury (CA, IV, 3317-61)

--Douglas L. Lepley

Ovid's account of Io's transformation
(Metamorphoses, I, 583-746) is a tale about the
suffering of an innocent maiden. Jupiter is enamored
by Io's beauty, but she rejects his advances. One day
in a forest under a cover of clouds Jupiter seizes Io
and rapes her. Seeing the unnatural cloud cover and
suspecting Jupiter's infidelity, Juno descends to earth
to catch Jupiter in his tryst. Jupiter, however,
senses Juno's approach and turns Io into a cow to
conceal his illicit deed. Juno's suspicions are
somewhat allayed by the trick, but, enchanted by the
cow's beauty, she asks to have it for a present.
Jupiter, knowing that to refuse such a trivial gift
will look suspicious, reluctantly gives Io to Juno.
Still fearing deception, Juno places Io in the custody
of the hundred-eyed Argus with whom Io finds life
miserable. She must eat bitter grass, drink muddy
water, and sleep on hard ground. When one day she
meets her father, she cannot even talk to him because
she can only low like a cow. After she writes her
bitter story in the sand with her foot, her father
laments her tragedy. As they mourn together, Argus
intervenes and drives Io away from her father. Unable
to watch Io suffer longer, Jupiter orders Mercury to
slay Argus. Mercury descends to earth and, disguised
as a shepherd, uses his pipes to lull Argus to sleep.
Mercury deepens Argus's slumber with a magic wand and
beheads him. Angered by the death of her watchman,
Juno torments Io who, fleeing to the Nile, falls on her
knees and begs Jupiter for mercy. Hearing her cries,
Jupiter pleads with Juno to end the punishment and
pledges his fidelity. Juno is appeased and Io is

45

restored to her former appearance.

Gower changes entirely the emphasis of Ovid's
narrative. Gower's tale is not about Io's suffering or
the feud between Jupiter and Juno. The lust of
Jupiter, the innocence and misery of Io, the protracted
enmity of Juno, the sorrow of Io's father--all of these
elements which dominate and unify Ovid's tale are
excluded from Gower's version. In fact, the events
which constitute the main plot of Ovid's account are
summarized by Gower in a short factual passage:

> Ovide telleth in his sawes,
> How Jupiter be olde dawes
> Lay be a Mayde, which Yo
> Was cleped, wherof that Juno
> His wif was wroth, and the goddesse
> Of Yo torneth the liknesse
> Into a cow, to gon theroute
> The large fieldes al aboute
> And gete hire mete upon the griene.
> (IV, 3317-26)

Furthermore, Gower places this summary at the beginning
of his tale and uses it simply to introduce his true
topic, the encounter between Argus and Mercury.

In Ovid's tale Argus and Mercury were minor
characters; their story was only a subplot used to
advance the main narrative. In Gower's version,
however, Argus and Mercury are major characters and the
encounter between Argus and Mercury is the central
action. While they were simply agents of the gods in
Ovid's account, in Gower's tale they act on their own
impulses. Consequently, they themselves determine
their own joy or grief. Gower clearly indicates that
the meaning of his narrative lies not in the
transformation of Io but in the outcome of the conflict
between Argus and Mercury.

It is evident, therefore, that in order to clarify
his purpose for telling his version, Gower consciously
changes the emphasis of Ovid's account. Rather than
dramatizing the plight of an innocent girl at the mercy
of capricious gods, Gower is intent on demonstrating
the dangers of sleeping when one should be awake. He
uses the tale of Argus and Mercury to show "That mochel
Slep doth ofte wo,/ Whan it is time forto wake" (IV,
3354-55). Gower suggests that a man who sleeps when he
should be alert may lose all he has, and that a man who
spends his life in somnolence controls his fortune no

more than if he were dead:

> For if a man this vice take,
> In Sompnolence and him delite,
> Men scholde upon his Dore wryte
> His epitaphe, as on his grave;
> For he to spille and noght to save
> Is schape, as thogh he were ded.
> (IV, 3356-61)

The world is filled with dangers, Gower says, and one must constantly be awake to avoid personal tragedies.

In addition to changing the emphasis of Ovid's tale, Gower also reshapes the roles of the important characters in his own version. In Ovid's account Io was a sympathetic character. She attempted to maintain her virtue by resisting the assaults of the lustful Jupiter. Jupiter was clearly the villian, Io the innocent victim. Gower eliminates any sympathy for Io. That Io rejects Jupiter's illicit love is deleted. That Jupiter can consummate his love for Io only by raping her is gone. Gower simply says that Jupiter lay beside Io and made love to her. He never mentions that she was pure or that she was an unwilling lover. Then, by having the injured Juno rather than Jupiter change her into a cow, Gower implies that Io's transformation is a consequence of her own actions. These changes reduce sympathy for Io. Because Gower eliminates the image of an innocent maiden who suffers terribly, the reader is not likely to care that Io is changed into a cow.

Furthermore, after Io's transformation, Gower never wants the reader to think of her as more than a cow. Through the rest of his story, Gower is careful to eliminate any details which might remind the reader of Io's humanity. Ovid showed that, although her body had been transformed, Io still had the mind of a human. He also heightened sympathy for Io by vividly dramatizing her suffering. In Gower, however, Io's horror over her transformation, her father's sorrow upon discovering her terrible fate, and her miserable life with Argus are gone. In Gower's account, Io is not driven about by the stern Argus as she was in Ovid's tale, nor does she have to eat bitter grass. Gower simply says that Io gets her meals "upon the griene" (IV, 3325), and walks beside Argus wherever he goes. In Gower's tale Io becomes simply an ordinary cow, an appropriate object for Mercury to steal from Argus.

47

By changing Io's role, Gower also is able to alter the roles of Argus and Mercury. A sympathetic Io in Ovid's tale made Argus a hateful character, a stern and shrewd guardian who perpetuated Io's suffering. By eliminating sympathy for Io, Gower reduces the reader's dislike of Argus. In Gower's tale Argus is not the agent of suffering he is in Ovid's account. Since Io has been reduced to nothing more than a cow, Argus becomes a simple rustic guarding his prize stock.

In fact, Gower creates some sympathy for Argus. While in Ovid's tale Argus was a supernatural creature who never slept, Gower makes him more human when he says that Argus "was selden wont to slepe" (IV, 3328). Argus, like an ordinary human being, must rest sometimes. When Gower says of Argus's eyes that "alle alyche wel thei syhen" (IV, 3330), he assigns an admirable trait to Argus. In Argus is located a value, seeing well, which must be upheld against villainy. The reader, consequently, supports Argus rather than opposes him. Finally, Gower makes Argus an unsuspecting victim who suffers from another man's treachery. Gower says that Argus is "beguiled" (IV, 3331). Wanting only to care for his cow, Argus is an inoffensive man who falls prey to the deceit of a thief and murderer.

Gower also alters Mercury's role. In Ovid's tale Mercury was the wing-footed god, descending from the heavens to rescue Io from her distress. By killing Argus, he performed an act of mercy. Gower changes Mercury from a divine savior into a common thief. Gone from Gower's tale are the description of Mercury's radiance in heaven, the divine sanction for the beheading of Argus, and the noble intent to rescue the suffering Io. In Gower's tale Mercury is introduced as a beguiler who is "affiled/ . . . to stele" (IV, 3332-33) Argus's cow. While in Ovid's tale Mercury stepped forth boldly and heroically to fulfill Jupiter's command, in Gower's version he "awaited/ His time" (IV, 3338-39) like a culprit slyly planning his misdeed. Mercury is further depicted as an enchanter who on his pipes plays "Thing which was slepi forto hiere" (IV, 3344). Having lulled Argus to sleep, he slays him, and "fot hot/ He stal the Cow which Argus kepte" (IV, 3350-51; italics mine). That Gower at this point chooses not to transform Io back to her former appearance de-emphasizes Mercury's role as savior and reinforces his characterization as mere cattle thief.

By remaking the characters, Gower provides Genius

with a clear case of a man who falls simply because he
is somnolent. While in Ovid's tale there was a sense
of justice in the beheading of Argus, in Gower's
version Argus is a sympathetic man who suffers only
because "he slepte" (IV, 3352) when he should have
been awake. Genius tells Amans that Argus was a "fol"
(IV, 3347) because he was "broght aslepe" (IV, 3347).
Had Argus been able to stay awake, he would have
avoided tragedy, but because he fell asleep, he lost
his awareness and control of the events around him and
was consequently destroyed. Genius is careful to point
out to Amans that when Argus fell asleep, "Ther was non
yhe mihte kepe/ His hed" (IV, 3348-49). The warning
that somnolence can be tragic is clear.

By changing the emphasis of the tale and by
remaking the characters, Gower successfully transforms
Ovid's account of the suffering of a maiden into a
lesson on the dangers of somnolence. Gower's version
of Ovid's tale clearly supports Genius's admonition to
Amans, and Gower's own admonition to the reader, to
"hold up thin hed,/ And let no Slep thin yhe englue,/
Bot whanne it is to resoun due" (IV, 3362-64). To be
alert is to avoid somnolence, and since somnolence is a
chamberlain to sloth, being awake is one way of
avoiding this larger sin. Gower's re-creation of the
tale of Argus and Mercury, therefore, encourages the
reader to conclude with Gower that because a man who
spends his time sleeping may lose all he has, including
his life, it is important to sleep only at the proper
times.

The Tale of Iphis and Araxarathen (CA, IV, 3515-3684)

--Nicolette Stasko

Ovid's account of the death of Iphis and the
transformation of Araxarathen (Metamorphoses, XIV, 698-
761) is at once moving and didactic. Iphis, who is
low born, chances one day to look upon the princess
Araxarathen and falls desperately in love with her. He
attempts to win her favor by sending her messages, by
currying favor with her servants, by decorating her
doorpost with flowers, by sleeping on her doorstep, and
by employing all manner of loving persuasions.
Araxarathen remains unyielding to his pathetic
entreaties. She scorns and mocks him, leaving him no
hope of ever satisfying his desire. Finally, in total
despair, Iphis hangs himself from Araxarathen's
doorpost rather than continue in his unrequited love.
When morning comes, members of the household find
Iphis's body and take it to his mother. On the way to
the burial, the funeral procession passes the house of
Araxarathen. The hard-hearted girl hears the funeral
march and, in a fleeting moment of pity, asks to see it
passing below. As she stands looking down on the
procession, the god of vengeance punishes her for her
cruelty. The coldness of her heart spreads throughout
her body, and she slowly turns to stone. The stone
statue of Araxarathen is kept at Salamis to remind
young girls of the possible consequences of their
cruelty.

Gower greatly expands and alters this story. The
first change he makes is to reverse the social
positions of the two main characters. Iphis is changed
from a man of low birth into a wealthy prince.
Araxarathen is changed from a princess to a poor but

51

virtuous maiden. This reversal not only brings the
story closer to the situation of Amans, who is a
courtly knight, but completely shifts the moral
emphasis of Ovid's account as well.

In Ovid's version the pathetic, poor, and humble
Iphis had no chance to win the beautiful princess. His
one-sided courtship was a long and arduous one, and in
the end he was totally rejected by her. Gower's Iphis,
on the other hand, is a rich and arrogant prince who
sets his heart on a girl below his station in life. As
Gower puts it:

> Of worldes good, he was soubgit
> To love, and put in such a plit,
> That he excedeth the mesure
> Of reson, that himself assure.
>   (IV, 3523-26)

Unlike Ovid, Gower holds little sympathy for Iphis
since his love for Araxarathen appears to be selfish,
lustful, and unreasonable: a mere royal whim.

Araxarathen's character reversal is equally
important. Ovid's Araxarathen was a cruel and arrogant
princess who mocked Iphis's pitiable love for her.
Gower's Araxarathen, however, is a very sympathetic
character. She is poor and of humble birth, but
determined to preserve her virginity: "And as sche
scholde, tok good hiede/ To save and kepe hir
wommanhiede" (IV, 3533-34). In Gower, Araxarathen's
resolution to remain a virgin justifies her rejection
of Iphis's advances.

The length of courtship in the two versions also
undergoes an important change. Gower greatly shortens
the time Iphis spends trying to win Araxarathen. The
Iphis of Ovid's account spent long hours and used every
method of courtship in an attempt to persuade the
princess to accept him. His despair and suicide were
thus understandable. In his speech preceding the
suicide he did not wallow in self-pity; rather, he
matter-of-factly stated that the lights of love and
life must be extinguished together. In comparison,
Gower's Iphis seems extremely hasty and rash. His
brief courtship of Araxarathen is given only one line
in the tale: "He yaf, he sende, he spak be mouthe"
(IV, 3537). When she rejects him, he immediately loses
heart, gives up all hope, and commits suicide. His
lengthy death speech is full of self-pity and
melodramatic hyperbole about the death of a king's son.

He seems almost to enjoy playing the part of the rejected lover. Far from portraying Iphis with sympathy, as Ovid did, Gower emphasizes his rashness and premature despair: "So that he caste his hope aweie,/ Withinne his herte and gan despeire" (IV, 3540-41).

Other important changes in Gower take place after the suicide of Iphis. In Ovid's version, Araxarathen slowly turned to stone while looking at the funeral procession, a fitting punishment for her cruelty and hardness of heart. In Gower's account, on the other hand, Araxarathen hears a commotion when the members of her household find Iphis's body the following morning. Even before she is told the reason for the outcry, she knows intuitively that Iphis has killed himself for love of her. She makes a lengthy speech, which did not appear at all in Ovid's version, lamenting his death and blaming herself for it. She prays to be punished for lacking compassion, and, knowing that she has caused a suicide, she no longer wishes to live: "And as I dede, do to me:/ For I ne dede no pite" (IV, 3627-28). Her prayers are answered, and she is struck dead. Her body turns to stone and is carried in a procession through the streets of the city until it is finally set over the grave of her dead lover.

Gower also adds the epitaph carved into the marble tablet at the grave. This epitaph allows him to re-emphasize the moral of the story. Although Araxarathen remains a sympathetic and virtuous character until the end, Gower suggests that she is "to hard" (IV, 3681) in her dealings with Iphis. While her goal, which is to preserve her virginity, is justified, her means of attaining it are not charitable. Gower says that it is not good for a woman to "soffren men to deie so" (IV, 3677). He reserves his main criticism in the epitaph, however, for Iphis. If Araxarathen is too hard, Iphis is "to neysshe" (IV, 3681), or too soft, for he despairs too easily. This last reference to despair leads into Genius's final statement to Amans about Sloth, the subject of Liber Quartus:

> It grieveth be diverse weie
> In desespeir a man to falle,
> Which is the laste branche of alle
> Of Slouthe, as thou hast herd devise.
>   (IV, 3686-89)

By a simple reversal of the social and moral positions of two main characters, and by the addition of significant details, Gower entirely changes the original theme of Ovid's story. By transforming a tale designed to encourage women to yield to their lovers' desires into one which criticizes men for despairing, Gower alters the tale of Iphis and Araxarathen to suit his own purposes and to provide a masterful conclusion to Liber Quartus in the <u>Confessio</u> <u>Amantis</u>.

The Tale of Midas (CA, V, 141-332)

--Judith C. G. Moran

Ovid's tale of Midas (Metamorphoses, XI, 85-145)
is a story of irresponsible kingship, of foolishness,
and of wasted opportunity. Midas, King of Phrygia, is
a former student of the Bacchic mysteries. Silenus, a
priest and tutor of Bacchus, is brought before him in a
drunken state. Recognizing the status of the priest,
the king welcomes a kindred spirit and entertains him
lavishly for a full ten days before returning him to
his master. A grateful Bacchus allows Midas to choose
his own reward. His choice of the power to turn all
that he touches into gold brings him great pleasure
until he finds it does indeed extend to all things,
food and drink as well. Faced with the certainty of
starvation, Midas abjectly confesses his sin and begs
to be relieved of the gift which has so suddenly become
a burden. He is mercifully returned to his former
condition, but still remains a foolish man whose
stupidity is destined to bring him misery again.

The Midas story is one of the few in the Confessio
Amantis which do not deal directly with love. It
stands in Liber Quintus as Gower's first story about
avarice, and, through two basic changes he makes, it
also becomes part of his pervasive treatment of the
responsibilities of kings. The two alterations are,
first, to make Midas a more sympathetic character and,
second, to show him not only recognizing his error, but
also genuinely repenting of his sin and profiting from
the experience.

First, Gower completely eliminates all association
between Midas and the rites of Bacchus, thereby

avoiding any unfavorable implications about the king's
motivation in helping Silenus. Indeed, Midas is not
identified with any interest or philosophy other than
that of being a gracious human being. Ovid's Midas
recognized Silenus as an influential personage with a
mutual faith in the same god, and treated him
accordingly. Gower's Midas has no spiritual or
fraternal connection with the drunken Silenus brought
before him. His sincere concern is motivated solely by
the desire to preserve an unworthy priest from public
humiliation:

> This courteis king, tok of him hiede,
> And bad that men him scholde lede
> Into a chambre forto kepe,
> Til he of leisir hadde slepe.
> (V, 155-58)

He does not entertain his guest with ten days of
hedonistic revels such as a follower of Bacchus would
delight in. Gower's compassionate king provides only
the normal courtesy of extending food and shelter to a
hapless stranger. The grateful Silenus gives Bacchus a
glowing report of his treatment at Midas's court.
Bacchus suspects "a vilenie" (V, 170) in such
unwarranted graciousness, but tells Midas to choose his
own reward "of worldes good" (V, 179).

Ovid's Bacchus put no restrictions on what Midas
might choose as his reward. When both the spiritual
and material worlds were opened to him, his choice was
immediate and unhesitating. Gower's Bacchus, however,
does limit the area of choice to worldly goods.
Perhaps the suspicious Bacchus fears that if he opens
the spiritual realm as well, Midas might well choose
something incompatible with the goals of the god of
wine. The choice, restricted as it is, presents an
important challenge to the highly respected leader.
Midas wisely deliberates on his choice at great length,
for he "was of his axinge in doute,/ And al the world
he caste aboute,/ What thing was best for his astat"
(V, 181-83). He debates each of the three most logical
worldly choices: "delit", "worschipe", and "profit"
(V, 187-88). This three-part deliberation is
completely original with Gower; there was no hint of
any thought but greed in Ovid's king. Gower's purpose,
again, is to reinforce Midas's moral character as well
as the lesson on avarice.

In his deliberations Midas decides that "delit" is
not a suitable choice, "For every joie bodily/ Schal

56

ende in wo" (V, 193-94), and is for that reason "no
siker avantage" (V, 192); "worschipe" is transitory and
"Ther is no certein forto winne" (V, 200); and of
"profits" he thinks:

> I not in what manere I scholde
> Of worldes good have sikernesse;
> For every thief upon richesse
> Awaiteth forto robbe and stele.
>   (V, 204-07)

Since nothing is certain, he concludes, "He can no
siker weie caste" (V, 221). Gower makes Midas
courteous, gracious, and morally aware, but also very
human. Though Midas succinctly analyzes the
consequences of all the natural choices of men and
clearly rejects them as unworthy, still, "ate laste/ He
fell upon the coveitise/ Of gold" (V, 222-24).
Thinking of how easily wealth may be lost, he next
wonders "Hou that he mihte his cause availe/ To gete
him gold withoute faile" (V, 229-30). Here, as with
Ovid's Midas, the possibility of certain wealth whose
increase he himself can control is irresistable.
Ovid's Midas was motivated solely by greed; Gower's
Midas, on the other hand, feels compelled to justify
his moral lapse. Gold does have the ability to
corrupt, but, he rationalizes, "gold can make of hate
love/ . . . and ryht of wrong" (V, 238-39). And so he
prays that Bacchus might give him gold, "bot he
excedeth/ Mesure more than him nedeth" (V, 247-48). He
has forgotten what he himself knew before rejecting
"profit" as a choice--that no man needs so much wordly
wealth:

> Yit hadde he bot o mannes del
> Toward himself, so as I thinke,
> Of clothinge and of mete and drinke,
> For more, outake vanite,
> Ther hath no lord in his degre.
>   (V, 212-16)

Bacchus grants the king's request for the ability
to turn whatever he touches into gold. Like Ovid's
Midas, he joyously tests his new skill until he becomes
hungry and finds that all he brings to his lips becomes
gold. Unlike Ovid's Midas, he immediately realizes the
moral implication of what he has done: "Thanne he syh/
Of Avarice the folie" (V, 288-89). He begs to be rid
of his power. His wish is granted, and:

He goth him hom the rihte weie
And liveth forth as he dede er,
And putte al Avarice afer,
And the richesse of gold despiseth,
And seith that mete and cloth sufficeth.
                    (V, 316-20)

Not only does Midas begin to live as he previously
had done, but he goes on to use his experience as the
basis for teaching his subjects to avoid his mistake.
Gower's message is that kingship is a trust. Kings may
be as vulnerable to human foibles as other men, but
their responsibility for moral leadership is clearly
defined. Even in striving for good, a king may be
temporarily "smite" (V, 265) with Avarice, as Midas
is, or with any other form of sin, but he is still
responsible. Unlike Ovid's Midas, Gower's is a good
king before he succumbs to the desire for gold. He
falls before the same temptation, but he subsequently
learns from his mistake and becomes a worthier king
because of it.

The Tale of Echo (CA, V, 4583-4652)

--Karl A. Zipf, Jr.

Ovid's story of the punishment of Echo
(Metamorphoses, III, 359-69) is little more than a
prologue to the story of Narcissus, with whom Echo
falls in love. The nymph Echo originally has a normal
voice and bodily shape. When Juno, however, is about
to catch the nymphs lying with her husband Jupiter on
the mountainside, Echo detains the goddess by an
unceasing flow of words so that the nymphs can escape.
Juno soon discovers Echo's plot and, to punish her,
curtails Echo's speech so that she can only repeat the
last words which she hears others speak. This explains
the natural phenomenon called the echo.

Gower takes this brief incident and expands it by
developing the character of Echo and by focusing
directly on her crime and punishment. He also makes
the story more relevant to his audience by giving it a
contemporary courtly setting rather than the natural
and supernatural setting it had in Ovid. Gower's Echo
is no longer a nymph, but a lady-in-waiting to Juno,
the queen. And Jupiter is no longer unfaithful in
Gower's account.

The principle change Gower makes, however, is to
alter the character of Echo so much that she bears but
faint resemblance to the highly sympathetic frustrated
lover of Narcissus that she was in the Metamorphoses.
Perhaps the primary reason for the change is to fit her
character and actions to a tale about "love-brokerage":

> Brocours of love that deceiven,
> No wonder is thogh thei receiven

```
       After the wrong that thei decerven;
       For whom as evere that thei serven
       And do plesance for a whyle,
       Yit ate laste here oghne guile
       Upon here oghne hed descendeth,
       Which god of his vengance sendeth.
                         (V, 4573-80)
```

Gower makes Echo a love-broker, an active procurer of
women for Jupiter. In Ovid she was not a love-broker.
She may even have had nothing to do with Jupiter, for
her chattering was designed to protect the other
nymphs, rather than Jupiter. Gower also makes Echo
more explicitly guilty of wrongdoing. She is said to
be "full of tricherie" (V, 4586), to have "no schame"
(V, 4592), and to be a "traiteresse" (V, 4620). She is
not, as in Ovid, merely another nymph, but a personal
servant to Juno. This causes her deception of Juno to
be a more serious crime, for she is disloyal to her
mistress: "With queinte wordes and with slyhe/ Blente
in such wise hir lady yhe" (V, 4593-94). Thus, she is
distinctly the villain of Gower's tale. Rather than
being the sympathetic victim of Juno's wrath, as she
was in Ovid, she is the unsympathetic traitoress who
fully deserves the just punishment she receives.

    To contrast the less sympathetic Echo, Gower makes
Juno a far more sympathetic character. Instead of
being the shrewish and wrathful wife she was in Ovid,
she is now the betrayed queen who discovers the
unfaithfulness of her husband and the disloyalty of her
servant. Her punishment of Echo is both just and fair.
Juno's meting out of justice is an interesting aspect
of Gower's tale, for fully half of Gower's account
concerns a discussion of the crime of love-brokerage
and the punishment for it. The middle section of the
tale is reminiscent of a courtroom scene. After the
guilty party is apprehended, the charges are read and
the evidence is presented:

```
       "O traiteresse, of which servise
       Hast thou thin oghne ladi served!
       . . . thou madest me to wene
       That myn housbonde trewe were,
       Whan that he loveth elleswhere."
                    (V, 4620-21, 4626-28)
```

Then comes the sentencing:

```
            "Nou is the day
       That I thi while aquite may;
```

60

And for thou hast to me conceled
That my lord hath with othre deled,
I schal thee sette in such a kende,
That evere unto the worldes ende
Al that thou hierest thou schalt telle,
And clappe it out as doth a belle."
                    (V, 4633-40)

And, in true medieval fashion, Gower has made the
punishment fit the crime. In Ovid's version, Echo's
punishment was to repeat only the end of all that she
heard and never initiate speech herself. In Gower,
where the crime is specifically said to be a crime of
concealment, or refusing to tell what she knew, Echo is
appropriately punished by being doomed to repeat all
that she hears. In addition, Echo is cast out from the
court to live in the woods, far from the blessings of
civilization. The wise judge Juno appropriately
conducts the trial and rationally dispenses justice.

Though Gower gives Jupiter only a minor role, he
specifically mentions one detail in support of his
moral purpose: that Jupiter is guilty of adultery.
Jupiter was also guilty of adultery in Ovid's account,
but Ovid did not think of Jupiter's actions as either
particularly criminal or particularly adulterous.
Jupiter was merely true to his own divine nature.
Gower, on the other hand, has Genius emphasize
Jupiter's unfaithfulness in his closing remarks to
Amans:

Forthi, if evere it so befalle,
That thou, mi Sone, amonges alle
Be wedded man, hold that thou hast,
For thanne al other love is wast.
O wif schal wel to thee suffise.
                    (V, 4653-57)

This addition helps to make the tale fit into the
overall topic of Liber Quintus, for having lovers other
than one's spouse is a form of avarice in love.

Gower extensively expands and alters the story of
Echo he has found in Ovid. He takes a brief
explanation of the origin of a natural phenomenon, the
echo, and develops it into a moralistic condemnation of
deceptive servants and adulterous husbands.

61

<u>The</u> <u>Tale</u> <u>of</u> <u>Tereus</u> (<u>CA</u>, V, 5551-6048)

--Douglas L. Lepley

Ovid's tale of Tereus and Philomela (<u>Metamorphoses</u>,
VI, 424-674) depicts a horrifying world of savage
passions and wanton revenge. Because Tereus, King of
Thrace, has saved Athens from a siege, he receives in
marriage Procne, the older daughter of the Athenian
king Pandion. After a wedding marred by foreboding
omens, the couple returns to Thrace, where they live
happily for five years. Procne then grows homesick for
her sister, Philomela, and coaxes Tereus to bring
Philomela to Thrace. Arriving at Pandion's court,
Tereus begins to explain the reason for the visit, but
he is interrupted by the entrance of Philomela, whose
beauty immediately arouses his passions. Tereus
persuades Pandion to allow Philomela to go to Thrace.
After they return to Thrace, Tereus secretly imprisons
Philomela and rapes her. When Philomela threatens to
reveal his crime, Tereus cuts out her tongue. Tereus
then returns to Procne and tells her that Philomela is
dead. Not being able to escape her prison or to tell
her tale, Philomela weaves her story into a cloth which
she has a servant deliver to Procne. Without Tereus's
knowledge, Procne releases her sister and plans a mad
revenge. Losing all sense of right and wrong, Procne
decides to get revenge on Tereus by killing Itys, their
son. Despite Itys's pleas, Procne and Philomela murder
him and cut him into pieces which Procne cooks and
serves to an unsuspecting Tereus. As Tereus eats his
son's flesh, Procne triumphantly reveals her demonic
revenge, and the blood-spattered Philomela thrusts
Itys's head before Tereus's face. Enraged, Tereus
tries to kill the sisters, but the gods prevent further
bloodshed by transforming all three people into birds.

63

Although Gower retains the essential plot line of
Ovid's tale, he mutes the horror of Ovid's gruesome
descriptions and reduces the detailed accounts of
Tereus's lust and Procne's mad desire for revenge.
While Ovid vividly described the mutilation of
Philomela and the dismembering and cooking of Itys,
Gower eliminates such gory images as Philomela's tongue
writhing on the floor and Itys's blood dripping from
the walls of Procne's room. Whereas Ovid gave a
detailed account of Tereus's inflamed passions, lustful
imaginations, and treachery, Gower gives only a brief
summary describing how the sight of Philomene (as he
spelled it) set Tereus's "herte on fyre" (V, 5622).
Gower also completely deletes Ovid's elaborate
description of Procne as a ferocious beast and demonic
avenger who, intent on torturing Tereus, confounds the
issues of right and wrong. Tereus's repeated assaults
on the mutilated Philomela, the wild Bacchic ceremony
Procne uses to cover the release of her sister, and the
roasting of Itys's flesh are gone from Gower's account.
By reducing Ovid's detailed dramatizations of inhuman
passions and wanton revenge, Gower changes the emphasis
of Ovid's tale. Rather than depicting the horror
caused by savage impulses, Gower creates a moral
exemplum which demonstrates that a man who takes love
by force is committing the sin of "ravine" and will
receive just retribution for his crime.

In addition to changing the emphasis of Ovid's
tale, Gower also alters the roles of the characters to
clarify his purpose for telling his own version. In
Ovid's account the three main characters were all
motivated by exaggerated desires and were all
villainous to some extent. In his rape and mutilation
of Philomela, Tereus seemed depraved, but in their
slaying and butchering of Itys, Procne and Philomela
seemed barbaric also. Gower, however, attempts to
create characters who have the normal impulses and
virtues of civilized people, and he tries to make a
clearer distinction between good characters and bad
ones.

Gower heightens Tereus's villainy. In Ovid's tale
Tereus's actions were governed by the abnormal nature
he inherited as a Thracian. Upon seeing Philomela for
the first time, Tereus immediately desired to rape her.
He responded instinctively, having apparently no
control over his actions. By eliminating any reference
to Tereus's abnormally impulsive nature, Gower enables
him to control his own deeds. In Gower's tale,
therefore, when Tereus rapes and mutilates Philomene,

he is morally responsible for his conduct.

To further heighten Tereus's accountability for his misdeeds, Gower makes Tereus less evil at the beginning of the tale. Pandion chooses Tereus for a son-in-law because he believes that Tereus is a "worthi king" (V, 5566) and "noble kniht" (V, 5567). Gower himself indicates that Tereus is a good husband truly devoted to Procne. When Tereus asks permission to take Philomene to Thrace, Pandion and his wife give their consent because they hold Tereus in "reverence" (V, 5608). At the start of Gower's tale, Tereus is a good man who might have chosen not to rape and mutilate Philomene. Suggesting that Tereus is aware of the moral implications of his actions, Gower shows that by assaulting Philomene, Tereus consciously chooses to indulge in wickedness.

Indeed, Gower does hold Tereus accountable for his misdeeds. Passing judgment on Tereus's rape of Philomene, Gower labels him a "tirant" (V, 5627) and a "ruide" knight (V, 5638) who has lost "alle grace" (V, 5630). The reader is told that Tereus's mutilation of Philomene is "a fieble dede of armes" (V, 5688). Because he has taken Philomene's virginity, Tereus is also judged a "raviner" (V, 5627). Finally, for his infidelity to Procne, he is called a "Spousebreche" (V, 6014). Gower shows that Tereus has violated the moral code by which men are judged worthy, that he is a knight who has sinned terribly.

Having made Tereus a villain, Gower recasts Procne and Philomela as woeful sisters who seek justice for the crimes committed against them. Gower initially arouses sympathy for Philomene and Procne by introducing the two women as members of an intimate and virtuous family that does not deserve to suffer. While Ovid never mentioned the sisters' mother, Gower completes the family circle by including an endearing mother who is concerned for her daughters' welfare. When Tereus rapes Philomene and is untrue to Procne, he seems a depraved tyrant who has brought tragedy to the innocent sisters and their loving parents. Furthermore, by having Philomene cry out to her father and mother when she is raped, Gower reminds the reader that Tereus's action will cause sorrow for the whole family. In Gower's tale, Tereus clearly becomes a villain, and Philomene and Procne are made innocent victims.

Indeed, throughout his narrative, Gower keeps
Philomene guiltless. While Ovid made Philomela a
deranged girl, mad for revenge, Gower keeps her
sympathetic. Whereas in Ovid's tale Philomela bitterly
threatened to avenge herself on Tereus, in Gower's
version she merely berates Tereus for his crime:

> "O thou of alle men the worste,
> Wher was ther evere man that dorste
> Do such a dede as thou hast do?"
> (V, 5655-57)

She calls Tereus a "false man" (V, 5676) and refers to
his act as a "felonie" (V, 5668). She accuses Tereus
of two crimes, taking her maidenhood and being
"untrewe" (V, 5681) to her sister. At her angriest
moment, Philomene accuses Tereus of being "mor cruel
than eny beste" (V, 5677). While animals mate to have
offspring, she says, Tereus cares not at all about
having children or about his marriage vows. He wants
only to fulfill his desires. Philomene shows that
Tereus is an unnatural man who has committed a heinous
crime, but she never mentions a desire for revenge.

After Tereus cuts out her tongue, Philomene remains
a sympathetic character. While Ovid described
Philomela's wrathful mind, madly focused on revenge,
Gower simply reports that Philomene made a prayer from
her "herte" (V, 5740). This prayer to Jupiter is one
of Gower's additions to Ovid's tale, and it shows
Philomene's resignation to the divine will. In her
prayer, she first refers to Tereus's "wrong doinge" (V,
5743). She laments the loss of "mi speche and mi
virginite" (V, 5749), emphasizing Tereus's role as a
raviner. Philomene shows that she has a right to be
vengeful, but finally she asks for vengeance only as an
act of Jupiter's will. She is not possessed by a mad
desire for revenge but asks only that Jupiter punish
Tereus for his crimes.

When the sisters finally are able to punish Tereus,
Gower is careful to keep Philomene's character
unblemished. Philomene does not take an active part in
the murder of Itys. Only Procne kills, butchers, and
cooks Itys. Philomene does help to set Itys's head
before Tereus, but Gower eliminates Ovid's description
of her as a blood-spattered, dishevelled, and deranged
girl. Gower is careful to keep Philomene the innocent
victim whose suffering heightens Tereus's cruelty.

Although he cannot keep Procne a purely innocent
character, Gower does minimize her cruelty and
emphasize her role as an agent of divine justice.
While Ovid described Procne as a ferocious tigress and
demonic avenger, Gower stresses her role as a sorrowing
sister and an injured wife. In describing Procne's
response to Tereus's report of Philomene's "death,"
Gower is careful to mention that Procne is "gentil and
kinde" (V, 5725) and deeply affected by the loss of
Philomene. When she is finally reunited with
Philomene, Procne is depicted as a woeful woman who
sorrows over the suffering of her sister and the
infidelity of Tereus.

     Procne's cruelty is further blunted by her two long
prayers. In her prayer to Venus and Cupid, she
emphasizes that she is a loyal wife and that Tereus is
an unfaithful husband and raviner. Procne indicates
that Tereus is the "unkinde" (V, 5836) man who has
done "wrong" (V, 5839). In her prayer to Apollo,
Procne again laments Philomene's tragedy and asks
Apollo to "do vengance of this debat" (V, 5847).
Trying to assume some guilt for her sister's
misfortune, she only reveals her own innocence and
further accentuates Tereus's treachery. She says that
she would forgive Tereus for a lesser sin, but,
concluding that Tereus has committed a crime which
cannot be forgiven, she knows she must seek justice.
She closes her prayer by asking the gods to sanctify
her punishment of Tereus. Procne's prayers reflect not
the ravings of a vengeful woman but a rational plea for
justice.

     Gower shows that his sympathy lies with the
sisters' cause when he notes that any man who heard
their prayers could not help but feel pity for them.
He also adds that Procne and Philomene are essentially
good women who were forced to commit their crime
because of the immoral actions of Tereus:

          Thes Sostres, that ben bothe felle,--
          And that was noght on hem along,
          Bot onliche on the grete wrong
          Which Tereus hem hadde do,--
          Thei schopen forto venge hem tho.
                         (V, 5880-84)

Gower also minimizes Procne's cruelty by indicating
that Procne kills Itys because she is "mad/ Of wo" (V,
5891-92). While to lose control of one's reason is
generally considered a sin in Gower's tale, the

vileness of Procne's deed is mitigated because she has acted out of sorrow for the injury done to her sister and to herself. Her motive makes her crime less malicious.

Gower intends the reader to remain sympathetic with Procne, as is clearly indicated by his alteration of the role of Itys. Whereas Ovid introduced Itys early in his tale, Gower does not introduce Itys until he is needed as a means for working revenge on Tereus. While Ovid aroused sympathy for Itys by describing his pleas for mercy, Gower says that Itys did not make a "noise or cry" (V, 5896) when Procne slew him. Whereas Ovid emphasized the horror of the murder of Itys by describing how Procne drove a sword into Itys's side and then cut his throat, Gower eliminates these descriptions. Gower reduces sympathy for Itys, not wanting the reader to think of Itys's murder as more than punishment for the raviner, Tereus.

That Procne is motivated by a desire for justice is reflected in what she says to Tereus after she has revealed her terrible deed. While Ovid merely recorded Procne's sinister glee over the success of her vengeance, Gower has her express her dissatisfaction in a direct speech chastizing Tereus for his crimes. Procne begins her speech by berating Tereus for being so cold-hearted that he feels no remorse for his misdeeds. She believes that Tereus is particularly evil because his conscience is not stirred by his guilt. Procne also identifies Tereus as a "raviner" (V, 5919) who has done shame to love both through his rape of Philomene and through his infidelity to Procne. Procne tells Tereus that he will be remembered only for his "defame" (V, 5925). The thrust of Procne's speech is that Tereus is a false man and a tyrant who suffers only because he has sinned. Whereas in Ovid's tale all of the characters were wicked, in Gower's version Tereus emerges as the villain, and Procne and Philomene become the defenders of morality.

To emphasize his judgments of the characters, Gower elaborates Ovid's account of their transformation into birds. While Ovid described only briefly each character's appearance as a bird, Gower gives a detailed account of each bird's habits and interprets the meanings of the songs of Procne and Philomene. The birds have traits corresponding to the personalities of the characters:

          Echon of hem in his degre
          Was torned into briddes kinde;
          Diverseliche, as men mai finde,
          After thastat that thei were inne.
                    (V, 5938-41)

Gower turns the disgraced Philomene into a bashful
nightingale who hides in the thickest part of the
forest. She laments the loss of her "maidenhiede" (V,
5955) and sings about the "wounde" (V, 5995) done to
her by a man in "lusti fievere" (V, 5995). She is
judged a blameless girl who has suffered unjustly.
Procne is turned into a swallow who spends her summers
singing about the infidelity of Tereus and flying near
houses to warn wives about "the falshod of hire
housebonde" (V, 6020). Gower is also careful to keep
Procne guiltless by eliminating Ovid's reference to the
spots of blood on her breast. Gower makes Procne a
loyal wife who is grievously injured by her unfaithful
husband. Quite appropriately, Tereus is changed into a
"lappewincke" (V, 6041), a bird with the reputation of
being the "falseste of alle" (V, 6047). Tereus is
clearly judged a corrupt man who has sinned against
Philomene's maidenhood and Procne's fidelity.

     By passing judgment on the characters as he has
remade them, Gower shows that he holds Procne and
Philomene nearly blameless for their actions. In the
moral context of his civilized world, Gower finds
Tereus the corrupted man who, by taking Philomene's
virginity, has proven himself an unfaithful husband and
raviner. Tereus sins against reason and nature. The
vicious punishment that he suffers at the hands of
Procne and Philomene is shown by Gower to be no more
than an act of justice sanctified by the gods. The
tale as Gower has remade it serves as a clear warning
that a man who indulges in ravine may be punished
horribly. Genius echoes Gower's warning when he says
to Amans:

          Bewar, mi Sone, er thee so falle;
          For if thou be of such covine,
          To gete of love be Ravine
          Thi last, it mai thee falle thus,
          As it befell of Tereus.
                    (V, 6048-52)

Showing that he has learned his lesson well, Amans says
that he will never take anything by force from his lady
and will receive only what is freely given.

                         69

The Tale of Neptune and Cornix (CA, V, 6145-6217)

--Natalie Epinger Ruyak

Ovid's account of the attempted seduction of Cornix by the sea god Neptune (Metamorphoses, II, 569-88) is related from Cornix's point of view. Cornix, a king's daughter, who has been wooed by many wealthy and worthy suitors, is so beautiful that Neptune falls in love with her as she strolls along the beach. When his attempts to win Cornix's love fail, Neptune decides to resort to force, and he pursues the maiden. As Cornix flees, she prays to the gods to help her. The maiden goddess Pallas takes pity on her and transforms her into a crow. Cornix discovers that dark, downy plumage is suddenly growing on her body, and she finds herself flying instead of running. As a crow, Cornix is appointed one of Pallas's attendants.

Gower considerably revises and expands Ovid's simple tale. First, Gower elicits considerable sympathy for Cornix by pitting her innocence against the corruption of Neptune. She is a beautiful chambermaid in Pallas's chambers instead of a king's daughter, as she was in Ovid's tale. Thus, it is because of the nature of her work and the justice of her cause, rather than her social position, that she can appeal successfully to the gods for help. Cornix's motivations are emphasized in Gower's version. Whereas Ovid did no more than imply that Cornix wanted to keep her virginity, Gower explicitly states it, because the moral purpose of his story hinges on it. Cornix begs Pallas to help her

71

"To kepe and save myn honour:
Help, that I lese noght mi flour,
Which nou under thi keie is loke."
                              (V, 6191-93)

Since Ovid did not stress Cornix's desire to keep her
virginity, her rejection of Neptune apparently resulted
from a personal dislike of him. Gower's Cornix,
however, prays intensely to save her virginity. She
prays to protect herself not from just one man, but
from all men. By portraying a woman so desirous of
maintaining her virginity that she will pray for its
preservation, Gower successfully elicits a sympathetic
response from the reader.

    Gower tells this story, which is designed to show
the ill effects of avarice in love, to warn
specifically against the stealing of maidenhood or
virginity. Genius sums up this warning to Amans at the
end of the tale:

        Mi Sone, be thou war therfore
        That thou no maidenhode stele,
        Wherof men sen deseses fele
        Aldai befalle in sondri wise.
                              (V, 6218-21)

Because Gower's purpose is to emphasize the sin of
stealing virginity, it is fitting that Gower transforms
rape into robbery. In Gower's version, Neptune hopes
to "fulfille his lust of Robberie" (V, 6187). To
emphasize Neptune's lust for sexual robbery, Gower
makes Neptune more explicitly vulgar and grasping than
he was in Ovid. Whereas Ovid stated merely that
Neptune fell in love, Gower describes the process as
one of a robber seeking to rob a maiden of her
treasure:

        And hire in bothe hise armes hente,
        And putte his hond toward the cofre,
        Wher forto robbe he made a profre,
        That lusti tresor forto stele,
        Which passeth othre goodes fele
        And cleped is the maidenhede,
        Which is the flour of wommanhede.
                              (V, 6176-82)

    There is no chase scene is Gower's tale, as there
was in Ovid's, for Neptune stands directly in Cornix's
way. As a result, instead of running, Cornix weeps
despairingly. This added detail makes the attempted

                        72

crime even more terrible, for Cornix's tears show that she is a passive and helpless female. Gower thus aptly stresses the severity of the crime and emphasizes his point about the evil of stealing virginity.

At the end of his tale Gower also adds the detail of Neptune's being scorned for his attempted "robbery":

> The faire Maide him hath ascaped,
> Wherof for evere he was bejaped
> And scorned of that he hath lore.
> (V, 6215-17)

Ovid, on the other hand, ended his tale abruptly after the transformation itself. Gower, no doubt, adds this element of reproach and shame both to reinforce Genius's warning to Amans and to prove that it is indeed wrong for a man to try to steal a woman's maidenhead.

One of the most impressive additions Gower makes to Ovid's version is the use of functional imagery. In transforming rape into robbery, Gower stresses that the attempted robbery is not just of Cornix's maidenhood but also of her maidenhead. Gower thus compares the maidenhead to a physical, tangible item. As a "lusti tresor" (V, 6179), it becomes something which can be readily stolen. Gower also compares the maidenhead to the "flour of wommanhede" (V, 6182). Cornix herself reveals just how precious this "flower" is when she refers to its being kept under Pallas's lock and key. Gower also draws an analogy between the maidenhead and precious jewelry, "the broches" and "the Ringes" (V, 6173). As the transformation occurs, Gower stresses that Cornix's maidenhead remains pure white: "Under the wede of fethers blake,/ In Perles whyte" (V, 6209-10).

Gower also cleverly adds to Ovid's account imagery related to hands and arms. This use of manual imagery is added to stress even further that what had been rape in Ovid's account is now a lustful robbery. In Ovid's version, Neptune did not touch Cornix, but in Gower's version, Neptune seizes Cornix with "bothe hise armes" (V, 6176) and extends "his hond toward the cofre" (V, 6177). Gower's addition of a mention of Mars to his tale complements this manual imagery, for Gower suggests that if Neptune had prayed to Mars, a god noted for his strength, he might have prevailed: "Withouten him may noght availe/ The stronge hond" (V, 6154-55). It is possible, of course, that Gower also

73

adds Mars to the tale to serve as a foil for Neptune. Mars's masculine drive seems to be properly channeled: first, he uses his strong hand in battle, not for robbery; second, because he is married to Pallas his gratification of sexual urges is acceptable, as it is clearly not for Neptune.

In short, Gower has transformed the tale of Neptune and Cornix from a tale about rape into one which effectively demonstrates the wrongness and the ill-effects of trying to steal love. Through it, Genius shows Amans that in love, as in other human relationships, avarice is sin.

The Tale of Leucothoe (CA, V, 6713-83)

--John B. Gaston

Ovid's story of the love of the sun god for the
mortal Leucothoe (Metamorphoses, IV, 190-270)
emphasizes the tragic cruelty of the girl's death.
Venus, in vengeance for the sun god's exposure of her
affair with Mars, causes Phoebus to fall in love with
Leucothoe, daughter of Orchamus and Eurynome. In order
to see her, he rises too soon and, to prolong his joy,
sets too late. His light fades and he grows pallid
from love. He forgets his former loves. One night,
while his horses graze in pasture, he enters
Leucothoe's room disguised as her mother. In this form
he steals a kiss and, sending the servants away,
reveals himself to her as Phoebus. The girl's fear at
his announcement enhances her beauty. He returns to
his true shape. Overcome by his glory, Leucothoe
submits to him without murmur. Clytie, a former love
of Phoebus, is furious. She jealously brings the
affair to the attention of Orchamus, who, enraged,
buries Leucothoe alive, despite her protestations that
she had been the unwilling victim of Phoebus's lust.
Phoebus exhumes her and tries to save her, but he is
too late; she is dead. He transforms her into a shrub
of incense. Clytie, abandoned by the god, wastes away
and finally is transformed into a sunflower, which
keeps its face always to the sun.

Gower makes several character alterations in his
version of this tale. The changes are almost all
designed to shift the blame for the rape as much as
possible onto the shoulders of Phoebus, and to
emphasize that his is a crime of stealth.

75

The roles of the women in the tale are altered slightly to emphasize Phoebus's guilt. In Ovid, Venus instigated Phoebus's love for Leucothoe as a means of getting revenge on him for exposing her affair with Mars. In Gower, on the other hand, because there is no reference to this revenge motive, it appears that Phoebus's lust for Leucothoe is motivated more by his own desires than by Venus's machinations. Leucothoe herself has a rather small role in Gower's version, but even here Gower makes a slight change by not suggesting, as Ovid did, that she had been a somewhat willing partner to the rape. Gower throws the full blame on Phoebus, rather than on any of the women involved in the case.

The character who undergoes the most extensive change is Phoebus himself. Gower makes his situation somewhat more applicable to the human situation of Amans by playing down Ovid's description of him as the sun god. Gower eliminates his dramatic revelation of his true identity to the girl, for example, thus also suggesting that he overcame the girl by force, rather than by impressing her with his unparalleled brilliance. More important, Gower greatly emphasizes Phoebus's stealth, for the tale is designed by Gower to demonstrate the evils of stealth, one of the aspects of avarice. Accordingly, Phoebus is said to lie in wait for a long time "lurkende upon his stelthe" (V, 6746) before he sneaks in "al sodeinliche" (V, 6750) to take Leucothoe's virginity. Gower also has his entrance take place during the daylight hours, rather than, as in Ovid, at night. This change is surprising when we recall that Phoebus (in Ovid at any rate) was the source of all daylight, and when we recall that Gower had earlier (e.g., V, 6507-08) discussed stealth as a sin especially suited to the night hours. Rather than detracting from the stealth, however, this change actually makes the act more stealthy by showing that Phoebus performs his act under the most difficult of circumstances: "And ek also brod dai it was,/ Whan Phebus such a Stelthe wroghte" (V, 6792-93).

Gower has reworked his tale, then, to create a more guilty Phoebus who uses stealth to achieve his immoral ends. He transforms Ovid's tale of tragic love and fearful vengeance into a moral exemplum on the evil effects of stealth as a means of achieving avarice in love. As he has done in his other tales adapted from the Metamorphoses, Gower shows us once again that he is in full control of his source materials, and that he adapts them skillfully and consistently to his own fourteenth-century moral purposes.

PART TWO

Gower's Transformation of the Birth of Alexander

Introduction to Part Two

It has long been known that, although in writing
his Tale of Nectanabus Gower relied primarily on Thomas
of Kent's Roman de toute Chevalerie, he also drew in
smaller ways on one or more earlier Latin sources. G.
C. Macaulay, for example, in The Works of John Gower,
Early English Text Society (Oxford, 1901), 3, 519-21,
discusses the question of Gower's sources for the story
of the circumstances surrounding the birth of
Alexander, as does George L. Hamilton, in "Studies in
the Sources of Gower," Journal of English and Germanic
Philosophy, 26 (1927), 491-520. Neither scholar,
however, discusses in much detail Gower's adaptation of
the material he found in either the Roman or the Latin
sources. The first chapter below is an attempt to
suggest more fully the essential originality of Gower's
version of the story. The subsequent chapters are
designed to make available to scholars who wish to
study the relationships among the various versions of
the story of Nectanabus convenient texts of two early
versions of the story with, on facing pages,
translations of them. All quotations from the Tale of
Nectanabus in the Confessio Amantis are taken from
G. C. Macaulay, The English Works of John Gower,
volume 2.

Diabolical Treachery in the Tale of Nectanabus

--Peter G. Beidler

There can be no doubt that, although he also probably picked up certain details from one or another Latin source, Gower learned the main outlines of the story of the birth of Alexander the Great from Thomas of Kent's Anglo-Norman Roman de toute Chevalerie. Even so, it must be emphasized that Gower's version of the story of the part which the sorcerer Nectanabus played in the seduction of Philip's Queen Olimpias and in the resulting birth of Alexander is by no means a translation into Middle English of Thomas of Kent's story. On the contrary, Gower shifts the orientation of the story almost completely and adapts it to his own moral and artistic purposes.

One category of change which Gower makes in the story serves to render it more comprehensible to a medieval audience. Gower's account of Olimpias's birthday celebration, for example, is considerably different from Thomas of Kent's. In the Roman de toute Chevalerie Olimpias's progress was accompanied by the blowing of trumpets. Gower expands this brief reference to the celebration festivities into a very fourteenth-century English passage:

> Ther was gret merthe on alle syde;
> Wher as sche passeth be the strete,
> Ther was ful many a tymber bete
> And many a maide carolende:
> And thus thurghout the toun pleiende
> This queene unto a pleine rod,
> Wher that sche hoved and abod

```
          To se diverse game pleie,
          The lusti folk jouste and tourneie.
                              (VI, 1842-50)
```

     To give another example, Gower changes Nectanabus's
magic by shifting the emphasis from witchcraft to
astrology. In the <u>Roman</u> <u>de</u> <u>toute</u> <u>Chevalerie</u> Nectanabus
conjured up the dream for Olimpias by mixing herbs and
intestines with his own blood, then sprinkled this
concoction, as he spoke certain charms, over a wax
image of Olimpias surrounded by candles. Gower, on the
other hand, very much plays down these witching
associations and adds astrological computations not
mentioned in the <u>Roman</u>. Skipping entirely the mixing
of his blood with other substances, Gower's Nectanabus
gets out his books:

```
          He loketh his equacions
          And ek the constellacions,
          He loketh the conjunccions,
          He loketh the recepcions,
          His signe, his houre, his ascendent,
          And drawth fortune of his assent.
                              (VI, 1959-64)
```

Gower's English audience took astrology very seriously,
but would have been puzzled by that other conjuring.

     In addition to making changes which would render
his story more comprehensible to a fourteenth-century
English audience, Gower simply omits certain aspects of
the Anglo-Norman story from his own retelling of it.
Sometimes he omits elements because they are confusing
or unnecessary. Gower omits, for example, Nectanabus's
prediction that Philip will abandon Olimpias and take
another wife. He omits Nectanabus's request than an
extra bed be placed in the castle for him so that he
can sleep there and stand ready to protect her should
she need it. Gower vastly simplifies the birth scene
by omitting Nectanabus's insistence that Olimpias
delay the birth--once so that the child will not be a
beggarly coward, and the second time so that it will
not be born half in the shape of a hog--and by omitting
Olimpias's screaming and straining to keep the child
from being born until the astrological setting is right
for it. The birth scene, and Nectanabus's part in it,
are much simpler in Gower:

```
          Nectanabus, in privete
          The time of his nativite
          Upon the constellacioun
```

Awaiteth, and relacion
Makth to the queene hou sche schal do.
(VI, 2251-55)

Similarly, Gower omits the lengthy account of
Alexander's taming of the magnificent horse Bucephalus.
Gower makes these omissions to simplify an
unnecessarily complex story and to focus his own
account of the story on what he considers to be more
important elements.

   To better understand what elements Gower considers
most important, let us examine the frame-story context
which Gower provides for this story in the Confessio
Amantis. Genius, the lover's confessor, is explaining
to Amans that some lovers will even turn to sorcery and
black magic to win their desires. Amans says that he
knows nothing of these arts, though if he had known
them he might have tried to used them to win his lady.
Genius replies that any man who tries to use sorcery
for that purpose will regret it in the end, and then he
tells Amans the Tale of Nectanabus to illustrate the
point. For Gower, then, the tale is an exemplum, a
tale designed to exemplify the specific moral point
that a man who uses sorcery to gain the love of a woman
will be sorry. The tale Gower found in the Roman de
toute Chevalerie had the potential for serving his
needs, but Gower found that he had to make a number of
changes in the plot and characterization to focus the
story more directly on the theme of punishment for
sorcerers who misuse their art for romantic purposes.
To be more specific, Gower found that in redoing his
source materials he was transforming the story of the
birth of Alexander into the story of the treachery of
Nectanabus.

   In accordance with this new focus for the tale,
Gower consistently darkens the character of the
sorcerer Nectanabus. Instead of coming to Olimpias to
tell what turns out to have been mostly a true
prediction, Gower's Nectanabus "feigneth with hise
wordes wise" (VI, 1901) his story about the god's
desire to impregnate her with a son. Queen Olimpias
believes to be true a prophecy which is only "guile and
Sorcerie" (VI, 1951). Instead of being a prophet,
then, Nectanabus is reduced to the status of a mere
"guilour" (VI, 2015, 2053, etc.) who uses "the deceipte
of his magique" (VI, 2061) to trick his victim:

        With guile he hath his love sped,
        With guile he cam into the bed,

85

With guile he goth him out ayein:
He was a schrewed chamberlein,
So to beguile a worthi queene.
                    (VI, 2095-99)

Gower makes it repeatedly plain that since Nectanabus
misuses his art to deceive innocent people he must be
punished. The beguiler will be beguiled, and poetic
justice is achieved when Alexander kills the evil
Nectanabus:

        Bot for o mis an other mys
        Was yolde, and so fulofte it is;
        Nectanabus his craft miswente,
        So it misfell him er he wente.
                    (VI, 2359-62)

By altering the focus of the plot, by changing the
characterization of the sorcerer, and by emphasizing
the justice of Alexander's murder of him, Gower
transforms the more neutral story in his source into a
piece of functional morality.

     Further to shift the focus of the moral censure to
Nectanabus, Gower consistently exonerates Queen
Olimpias. This shift is most obvious right at the
start of the tale in the account of the birthday
celebration. Olimpias in the Roman seductively and
immodestly displayed her charms. She made a birthday
procession through town specifically to show off her
body. She wore a scarlet robe and was bedecked in
expensive jewelry. After awhile she removed her robe.
Nectanabus saw her beauties thus on display and was
captivated. Gower significantly changes all this. His
Olimpias does not ride out for the purpose of
displaying her body. Far from being dressed in gaudy,
expensive, or revealing dress, she is said to be
dressed simply "in good arrai" (VI, 1834). She does
not remove any of her clothing. Gower's changes are
very important, for it is clear that his Olimpias does
not seek lustful looks from the men in the city.
Instead of her being responsible for Nectanabus's
lusting for her, all of the blame for this falls
directly on Nectanabus. Instead of reacting with a
normal lustful response to an immodest exhibitionist,
Gower's Nectanabus is guilty of lusting after a modest
woman who has not sought to tease him with her physical
charms. Similarly, when Nectanabus later joins her at
the palace for their second interview, Gower's Olimpias
does not, as Thomas's had, recline seductively on a bed
as she talks with him. Gower wants the lustful

86

thoughts and actions to be Nectanabus's, not
Olimpias's.

Numerous other small changes reinforce this initial
shift in the character of Olimpias. In the Roman de
toute Chevalerie, for example, she petulantly
interrupted Nectanabus's lecture about the planets to
ask him about her own destiny; in Gower's version, on
the other hand, Olimpias "sat stille and herde what he
wolde" (VI, 1899). In the Roman, Olimpias blushed when
she took off her robe before the admiring gazes of the
men; in Gower's version, where she never does so
disrobe, she blushes instead when Nectanabus tells her
that she must allow the god to make love to her. In
the Roman, Olimpias foolishly never doubted
Nectanabus's words or intentions; in Gower's version,
she is rightly suspicious and says she will not believe
him until she sees "a betre prieve" (VI, 1924), a
"proof" which Nectanabus provides in the form of a
dream. In the Roman, Olimpias actively enjoyed making
love with the "god" and, saying that she valued the
love of a god more than that of a knight, asked
Nectanabus when her new lover would return to console
her again; in Gower's version, this becomes a simple
question when she asks Nectanabus "if that this god
nomore/ Wol come ayein" (VI, 2109-10). In the Roman,
only after her pregnancy began to show did Olimpias
express her concern about her husband's suspicions; in
Gower's version she expresses her concern immediately
after her sexual encounter with the "god." In the
Roman, Olimpias was afraid that her husband would kill
her when he returned to find her pregnant; in Gower's
version she is concerned not about her own life but
about her marital harmony with Philip:

> Hou sche schal stonden in acord
> With king Philippe hire oghne lord,
> Whan he comth hom.
> (VI, 2111-13)

These details all add up to a major shift in the
characterization of Queen Olimpias. Instead of being
the promiscuous seductress she was in Thomas of Kent's
story, she is a modest and faithful wife, participating
in an adulterous union only because she is instructed
to do so by a deceitful sorcerer who seems to be acting
with divine authority. Clearly, one reason for Gower's
transforming the seductress into a "noble gentil
queene" (VI, 2056) is to make her a more appropriate
parallel to Aman's own beloved. Another reason is
to darken further the character of Nectanabus. That

87

this is no promiscuous hussy, but a chaste and modest woman, makes his misuse of his sorcerer's art especially blameworthy and makes his final punishment especially appropriate. I would like to suggest, however, that Gower may have still another reason for so consistently ennobling the character of Olimpias.

Is it too outrageous to suggest that Gower may be writing in the Tale of Nectanabus a kind of rough parallel to the New Testament stories of the Annunciation and of Christ's birth? Consider the parallels: a married woman is visited by a being with supernatural powers and is told that she is to bear and give birth to a magnificent son, one who will rule the world. She doubts and fears this prediction, but is soon convinced that she is indeed destined to be the earthly mother of the son of a deity. Surely, the parallels are not exact. To mention only the most obvious lack of parallelism, Nectanabus, especially as Gower portrays him, is a poor excuse for the Gabriel who announces to Mary that the Holy Ghost will come to her and leave her pregnant with the Son of God. Still, there are enough parallels which do fit the biblical story that it seems entirely possible that a medieval audience steeped in Christian thinking might well have noted them.

Some of Gower's alterations of his source materials in the Roman de toute Chevalerie serve to reinforce the parallels between his and the biblical narrative. Most obvious, of course, are the many changes Gower made to improve the character of Olimpias. The promiscuous and voluptuous Olimpias in the Roman would have been unthinkable as a parallel to Mary, but the chaste queen of Gower's tale is not. Indeed, the adjectives which Gower uses to describe her sound distinctively Marian in their connotations: "mylde" (VI, 1918); "innocent" (VI, 1978); "noble" (VI, 2056); "gentil" (VI, 2056); "worthi" (VI, 2099); "withoute guile" (VI, 2284).

There are several supernatural elements in Gower's story which he may have added in a conscious effort to develop parallels with the story of the birth of Christ. For example, the dream which Olimpias has of a dragon who turns into a man at her bedside is more fully developed in the English version. Specifically, Gower adds the magnificent light "fro the hevene" (VI, 1981) which makes Olimpias's chamber bright, and adds the details that the dragon's scales "schynen as the Sonne" (VI, 1985). This heavenly brightness was not present in the Roman.

We have already seen that by eliminating the twice-postponed birth of Olimpias's child, Gower simplified his story. In so doing, of course, he also made his version of the birth closer to the story of Christ's birth. Gower also made other changes which suggest that his Alexander may be an intentional parallel to Christ. Although the Nectanabus in the Roman said that the father of Olimpias's future child was a god, in Gower's version Nectanabus says the child will also be a god:

> "Alle erthli kinges schull him drede,
> And in such wise, I you behote,
> The god of erthe he shal be hote."
>   (VI, 1938-40)

Gower could have picked up in the Roman the idea for a parallel between Alexander and Christ (see line 477 in the next chapter), but he did far more with that suggestion. After his Olimpias has conceived, for example, we are told that:

> Althogh sche were in part deceived,
> Yit for al that sche hath conceived
> The worthieste of alle kiththe,
> Which evere was tofore or siththe
> Of conqueste and chivalerie;
> So that thurgh guile and Sorcerie
> Ther was that noble knyht begunne,
> Which al the world hath after wunne.
>   (VI, 2085-92)

Even though Alexander is here spoken of as a knight rather than as a god, he is still referred to with superlatives ("the worthieste of alle kiththe") unmatched in the Roman.

It would be idle to point out possible parallels between Gower's story of the birth of Alexander and the story of the birth of Christ without attempting to explain why Gower might have developed the parallels. The most obvious reason, of course, is that such parallels enhance the stature of Alexander, recognized in the Middle Ages as perhaps the greatest of leaders before Christ. By suggesting that the circumstances at his birth were similar to those at Christ's, Gower makes him unusually special and helps to justify spending so many thousands of lines in Liber Septimus of the Confessio Amantis on his education at the hands of Aristotle. Gower may also have wanted to remind his audience that, just as Alexander overcame Nectanabus, so Christ overcame Satan. It is no accident, in this

89

connection, that Gower specifically compares Nectanabus
to Satan by suggesting that when Nectanabus "for lust
his god refuseth," he "tok him to the dieules craft"
(VI, 2344-45). Because of Nectanabus's unworthy
actions, God

> Ferst him exilede out of londe
> Which was his oghne, and from a king
> Made him to ben an underling.
> (VI, 2348-50)

It may not be reaching too far to see in that
statement--not present in the Roman--Gower's drawing a
conscious parallel to God's banishment of the Archangel
from heaven.

     In any case, it is clear that Gower is no slavish
imitator of his sources. With great originality and
with a clear sense of the artistic and moralistic needs
of his own story, Gower carefully selects from his
source materials, and carefully adds to them, to create
in the Tale of Nectanabus a story which shows clearly
that lovers who try to use evil methods to corrupt good
women will be punished, both in this life and in the
next.

Thomas of Kent's Account of the Birth of Alexander: Text and Translation

--Patricia Innerbichler De Bellis

Unfortunately, many of Gower's sources are not available in either modern editions or in translation. As a result, the full measure of Gower's originality is too little known. What follows is an attempt to help remedy this situation by presenting the text of one of Gower's sources for the Tale of Nectanabus along with a facing translation of it. My translation is neither rigidly literal nor poetic. I have attempted, rather, to convey the primary sense of the story line in modern English prose. The text of Thomas's story is taken from Paul Meyer's *Alexander le Grand dans la Litterature Francaise du Moyen Age* (Paris, 1886), pp. 195-221. Meyer's critical apparatus, which is not necessary for the purposes of this source book, has been deleted. Scholars are referred to his edition for his textual remarks and notes. I have, however, included in the text of the poem Meyer's notations which indicate readings from the "D" manuscript, as well as his suggested additions [in square brackets] and deletions (in parentheses). Some of his suggested emendations are for the sake of meaning; others are for the meter.

THOMAS DE KENT

EXTRAITS,

D'APRES LE MS. DE PARIS

———————

Ci comence le prologe en la geste de Alisandre.

Mult par est icest(e) siecle dolenz e perilleus,
Fors à icels qui servent le hault rei glorius
Qui por nus delivra le seon sanc precius;
Si cum mestier nus est eiet mercit de nus!   4
Car vie de homme est breve & icest(e) mund(e) laborus,
Decevables à tuz e à mulz enuius.
Nequident n'ad el siecle si bosoingnus
Qe alcun delit n'i ait itant meseurus.
Mult (par) poet estre dolent al jugement irus,
Al jur que tant avera tristes e poür[u]s   10
Qi pur sa char norir est en (i)cest mund penus;
A ceo que homme entent est sis quo[r]s desirus.
Un deduit ai choisi qi mult est delitus,
As tristes [D. est] confort e joie as dolerus
E assuagement as mals des amerus.   15
Deliter s'i poent homme ben chevalerus
E tuit ceo qi de romanz sunt coveitus.
A l'enviouse gent sunt li bon vers custus,
Car joie e enveisure est doel as envious.
Le mal le tient al quor, dunt vient le dit custus;   20
Altrement creveroit car tut est venimus.
Si nul d'els me reprent, seigneurs, tant di à vous:
L'ume mesprent sovent en outre mal grevus.
Mult par serreit li homme en ses fez eürus
Si à la fiée n'est repris des envious.   25

92

THOMAS OF KENT

EXTRACTS

From the Paris Manuscript

The prologue to the Tale of Alexander.

Much pain and peril exist in this century,
except for those who serve the high and glorious
King who delivered his own precious blood for our
sake. As he served us so does he deserve our
thanks, for man's life in this world is brief,
painful, deceitful, and wearisome. Never before
has the century had more need of distraction to
help overcome so much unhappiness. Many a poet is
saddened and bothered by the fact that so many in
this world must be miserable and fearful of the
mere task of survival. For those who will listen
and thus receive all that their hearts desire, I
have chosen a delightful story that will cheer
your sadness, alleviate your pain, and ease your
sorrows. Enjoy, if you can, good knight and all
those desirous of a story. Joy to the fortunate
few accustomed to good verse, and to the old for
whom good verse is a comfort; otherwise they would
die from everything poisonous. If none of you
criticize me, sirs, I will delight you with my
tale. One can often sympathize with another's
terrible sorrow.

Ore poet qui voelt oïr un vers merveillus
D'Alixandre le rei, de Darie l'orguillus,
Qi Babiloine prist e sis uncles Cyrrus.
Alixandre conquist itanz isles hidus,
Ynde & Ethiope, les regnes plentivus,   30
Par force de bataille en maint estur dotus,
Cum l'estorie dirrat, fort fu et vig[o]rous,
Hardi e conquerant [D. sages] e enginnus.

Lisage homme a[n]cien mesurerent le mounde,(b)   34
Cum le firmament turne e [D. cum] la terre est rounde;
En treis la departirent sanz compas, sanz espounde.
L'une partie est Asye, Affrike la secunde;
Europe est la tierz, de toz biens est fecunde.
Doze signes ad el ciel dont clarté nus habunde,
[D. Le curs des esteilles, cum la mer est parfonde;   40
Des doze mois parlerent e del vent que rebonde,]
E de marz e d'avril e de mai le plus munde,
De jung e de jungnet où Virgo se vergonde,
De aoust e de septembre [D. que sa veigne feconde,
De octobre e de novembre,] decembre od la fonde,   45
De Genver e de Fevrer, de quareme od l'onde.
Qi de cest plus querra (querge) que l'en responde.

De Nectanabus le rei de Lydie.

D'iceste chose esprover furent plusor baron.
Le plus sage de tuz Nectanabus od noun,
Qi le curs as planetes esprova par raison.   50
Tut li quarte element lui furent à bandon,
Quant altre rei conquist à force d'esperon
Dunt se combateit cist par estellacion;
Ne voulet guerreier se par artimage non.
S'alcons reis se presist [D. en]vers sa region,   55
Lores s'alast cocher segur en sa maison,
Ewe en un baçin presist ou en pocion,
E de sire feïst une conjunccion
Et en semblant de ceus, par machinacion;
L'une sembla[s]t à lui, l'autre à son compaignon;   60
En checun escrivoit dunc son propre non,
Combatre les fesoit par simulacion;
Ja tant ne venissent en chalam n'en dromun
Par engin nes tornast touz en destruccion.
Issi out tut dis pes dès qu'al tens Phelippon.   65
Avint que .xxx. reis, tut en un[e] saison,
Se pristrent contre [lui] por iceste acheison;
Sa mort eurent juré par mult grant traïson;
Out aveient mandé par meinte nation.   69
Quant (il) sout par les esteilles la lour entencion(c)
Un ris gitat de joie e dist une oreisun;

94

Now he who wishes can hear the wonderful story of
Alexander the King, the pride of Darius, who took
Babylon while his uncles took Cyrrus. Alexander
conquered by force so many islands and realms
(India and Ethiopia), and in battle took much
profit. As the story will tell, he was strong,
vigorous, bold, victorious, and resourceful.

Wise old men measured the world by the way the
round earth turns. They divided it into three
parts without the aid of a compass. One part was
Asia; the second was Africa; Europe was the third
and full of goodness. The sky which gave us
abundant light had twelve signs. Those wise men
spoke of the course of the stars; how deep the
ocean was; of the twleve months and of the
rebounding wind; of March and April and May, full
of life; of June and July where Virgo blushed with
shame; of August and September with their fertile
vineyards; of October and November, and December
at the end; of January and February; of Lent which
followed in the wake. And to any question one
asked they gave answers.

Of Nectanabus, King of Lybia.

Many barons were convinced that the wisest of
all these men was Nectanabus, who proved the
course of the stars by reason. All four elements
were at his disposal. While other kings conquered
by force of the sword, this one used sorcery and
refused any other arms. If some king threatened
his kingdom, he would retire to safety in his home.
He would, in a basin, place a potion. And he
would by machination make a mixture resembling
that king and another mixture resembling his
companion. On each he would write their names and
make them fight each other in a mock battle. Now,
not many came, for they would all be destroyed.
Such stories were told by all during Philip's
time. It came to pass that thirty kings all at
once warred against Nectanabus and swore to kill
him for high treason. The word was sent out to
many countries. When he, by way of the stars,
discovered their intention, he burst out in joyous
laughter and said a prayer.

Une charme en chaldeu, ne sai pas le jargoun;
Cil le fist dunc mettre en un bacin de latun;
Ses ymages moilla, (&) destempra sa puison,
Fist [lores] e dist charmes en estrange sermon.   75
Quant il out fest ceo q'il volt par sa conjureison
Idunc vit de son regne tote la confundeison;
S'il ne fuit n'i entent nule defension,
De la gent del realme nule gareison,
Tuz sunt pris e occis e mené en prison;   80
Bien veit, s'il i atent, jà n'aurat r[a]ançon.
D'atendre ou de l'aler ert en grant suspecion.
Quant il out tut pensé si s'en fut à larron,
Le chiez reis e tondu (e) vait en chaitiveison.

Coment Nectanabus s'en fuï e vint en Macedoine.

Nectanabus se out rés e deguisé s'esteit,   85
Fuit s'en de son regné que conneü ne seit.
Par peine, par travail eire mult par espleit;
A Macedoine en vient à la cité tut dreit;
En mult divers pensers ert sis quors en destreit;
Ne solt q[ue] il poet faire, ne quel mester fereit,   90
S'alcons hom(me) li demande, que respondre porreit.
Al derain s'en est porpensé e dit q'il se tendreit
A l'art d'astronomie qe il [le] plus saveit.
Un astralabe d'or od lui porté aveit,
La haltur en comprent des esteilles qu'il veit.   95

De la reine de Macedoine.

Or est Nectanabus à dreit port arrivé,
Ke li reis Phelippun n'ert pas en la cité,
Einz ert alé en ost où mult a demoré;
Reïne Olimpias governoit le regnee.
Ceo fu en avril en l'entrant d'esté   100
Cum cil bois sunt foillu, flori e borguné,
E chantent cil oisel ke l'iver ont passé;
Tote rien s'esjoïst fors cil desnaturé.
Grant feste tint la dame de sa nativité.
Quant il orent mangé les tables sunt levé.   105
Seignurs vous savez bien, sovent est [re]conté,
Dame coveite mult aveir los de belté,
Cel desire q'aveir los de honesteté.
Ceste se porpensa que sis corps est mostré,
Ja [dans] cent mile jur[s] poet bien estre loé;   110
Escria mareschals, chevalers ad mandé;
En poi d'ore [en] i out plus de mil assemblé.
Un blanc mulet d'Affrike si li ont amené;

A curse does not work in a caldron, so he placed it in a pewter basin. He moistened the images and added the poison, then recited the curse in a strange sermon. When he had accomplished what he wanted by way of incantation, he saw that his kingdom would be in total confusion if he did not flee or defend himself. He would receive no aid from the people, for they had all been taken to prison and killed. He understood that, if he remained, there would be no one to ransom him. To wait or to remain was the great question. When he had weighed all possibilities, the newly tonsured king fled like a thief into hiding.

How Nectanabus fled and came to Macedonia.

Nectanabus shaved to disguise himself and fled his reign without anyone knowing. With difficulty and effort he travelled very fast. He went straight to the city of Macedonia, with many different thoughts and a heart in distress. He could not make a decision about what trade he should follow. If someone should ask him, what could he answer? Finally he decided that he would stay with astronomy, about which he knew most. He had brought with him a golden astrolabe which reached to the visible stars.

Of the Queen of Macedonia.

As soon as Nectanabus arrived at the port, he learned that King Philip was not in the city. Philip had gone to the East some time before. Queen Olimpias governed the kingdom. This was in April, near the beginning of summer when the woods were in bloom, when summer flowers were budding, when the birds sang the passing of winter, and when everything, save the unnatural, rejoiced. The queen gave a great birthday celebration. When all had eaten, the tables were cleared. Sirs, as you well know, women very much enjoy praise of their beauty, especially if they are honest praises. So the queen decided to show her body, which could certainly be well praised if one had a hundred thousand days. She invited marshalls and knights and in a few hours there were more than a thousand assembled. A white mule from Africa carried her.

Mult ert bels e bien fet, un poi ert pomelé;   114
Curteise aveit l'eschine, tendre est par le costé,
E les jambes ot plates & le pié bien culpé.
Riche sele i aveit e arçoun bien peeré,
Saphirs e esmeragdes à compas ordené;
Covert fu d'un samit vermail, memiré;
Suscele i out de meisme à orfreis endenté.   120
Li estré furent d'or, [li] peitral tulpiné,
E sonez plus de mil [de] fin or esmeré.
Li frains fu de fin or entaillé e veillé
E les resnes de seie à gros botons doré.
La dame munte sus, li altre sunt monté,   125
E tint sur son poing [destre] un esperver mué
Quatre cornur maistre ount sun eire torné.
Li baron de la vile ont les chemins parré
Estendu ont lor pailes suz les piez tapiné,
E tymbres e tabours ont e leur corns corné.   130
N'en i ad nul si riche n'ait la dame encliné,
Agenulez à (la) terre trestuz desafublé;
E puis l'en sivient tut [par] defors la cité.
De tanz maneres gens unt dunc alevé,
Ces leons et ces urs e ces vealtres hué,   135
Itant (tant) bel juvencel se sunt el champ mellé
Li un sunt escherni li altre boürdé;
Maint bliaut de samit fut le jur deciré,
Maint dansel abatu, meint cheval reversé;
Plus de mil damoisels ount le jur karolé;   140
Li bobanz fu(s)t pur els mult greigneur demené.
Reïne Olimpias out sun mantel osté,
Mult fut gente de corps, le vis out coluré;
Bloi peil out e bien long, laschement galoné,
Un cercel d'or out sur sun chief posé,   145
Le vis aveit tartiz, le bras dreiz e quarré,
Blanche char come neif, le sanc i ot mellé.
En un poupre blialt fut sis corps freselé.
Plus gent corps ne mielz fait ne fut de mere né.
Nectanabus la veit, tut en est respensee;   150
En la bealté de li sunt si oil aresté.
Olimpias le veit, si l'ad mult avisé,
Estrange li sembla pur ceo qu'il est cusé,
As garnemenz q'il ad bien semble home desvé.
Du[n]t il seit e quels oem lui a puis demandé.   155
Quant il o[ï]t la dame de respondre ad doté;
Pensse, s[e] il demore, à mal lui ert torné,
Et dit: "Venu vus sui dire une verité."
La dame out brief respons à coe qu'il out parlé;
Poür out del vassal, ne sot sa volenté,   160
E volt que s'il siet de li rien, qu'il seit celé;
Ne [li] volt avant querre si ne seit en privé,
Kar desvé home ad tost à un ver asené.
Dunc montat la reïne el mul bien atorné,

She was beautiful and well built, and wore little
make up. She stood very properly. Her waist was
flat, her legs were long, and her feet were
delicate. She had a richly covered saddle and a
well-carved crest, adorned with sapphires and
emeralds made to order. She was covered with a
scarlet velvet cloth. Her saddle was of wrought
gold. The horse too was golden, his hooves of
iron. And more than a thousand bells of fine gold
rang out. The reins were of fine sculpted gold.
The lady mounted as did everyone else. She held
on her right fist a muted falcon. There was much
blowing of trumpets and bowing of heads as she
walked through the crowd. Four master trumpeters
sounded her passage. The village baron had her
path decorated and spread a carpet beneath her
covered feet. No one there had ever bowed before
such a lady. They all knelt down absolutely
stunned, then followed her out of the city
shouting out from all directions. Lions, bears,
and dogs appeared, as well as handsome young men
who romped in the field. Some fenced and others
jousted. Many a tunic was torn that day, many a
young man was defeated, many a horse was
overturned. More than a thousand young damsels
enjoyed themselves, dancing the whole day long.
For them the feast was very grandly led. Queen
Olimpias took off her robe. Her body was very
fine, and she blushed. She had long blond hair
ornamented with gold threads. A golden crown was
set upon her head. Her face was dark, her arms
straight and even. Her skin was like white snow
with red blood mixed therein. She was wrapped in
a purple tunic. Never had any woman a finer body.
Nectanabus saw her and all of him reacted. His
eyes were stopped by her beauty. Olimpias saw
him, and she too stared at him. He seemed strange
to her in his sewn garments, as if he were a
derelict. "By the course of the planets," he
thought, "I have often conquered; I have no other
charm for this is all I need." She asked him what
manner of man he was and from whence he came.
When he heard the lady he was afraid to answer and
thought he would be punished if he stayed. He
said, "I came to tell you a truth." The lady
answered him briefly, asking him to tell her what
he would, but he refused unless it was in private.
She gave him an appointment. Then, mounting her

E (si) s'en vint el palais quant assez out jué.
La dame est en son lit, n'ad le dit oblié;
Par un son chamberleint ad le vassal mandé.

De la belté de li fut li mestres suspris;
De devant la reïne est en son siege asis.
Olimpias li dist: "De vus ai tant enquis   170
"Q'astronomiens estes & des ars poestis;
"Or(e) me di[tes], bel mestre, où a[vé]s tant apris?
--Ohi," fait il, "reïne, une rien vus devis:
"Plus savez vous sul de l'art ke hom(e) ke unc fu vis;
"L'aventure sai dire chascune del païs,   175
"Espundre tuz sunges, tuz genz, tuz ris
"Ne de sort ne de charme nen est mi quers eschis;
"Del tur del firmament avons e los e pris,
"Par le curs des planetes ai meint avoir cunquis,
"Jee n[en] ai altre charme kar par ce me garis,   180
"E si est [i]coe l'art dont joe ai plus apris."
Olimpias li dit: "Or(e) me di, bels amis.
"A quei m'esgardas tu tut en [cest] jor el vis?
--Bele dame," fet il, "ne vus est unke (de) pis;
"Joe record le veir [dist] dunt joe ainz vous dis: 185
"En Egypte, ù ere qant joe de cest art lis,
"El temple à tuz les deus un sacrefice fis;
"Un respons i oï por quei sui ça tramis:
"Verité vus dei dire si cum joe vous pramis;
"Vous me conseillerez solung le vostre avis.   190
"Gré me devez savir qant joe vus [en] garnis."

La dame s'est acutée à l'esponde del lit,
Sengle en sa chemise, en un mantel samit,
Un cercel d'or el chief à ovre bon eslit;
Veit vestu le vassal en mult estrange abit   195
De ses diz pensive iest e mult forment s'en rit.
Il l'esgarda(s)t el vis, ne l'aime pas petit;
Danger fait de parler kar il volt que l'en prit;
El demorer illoec ad il mult grant delit.
En unes tables d'or une lecon li lit,   200
Les curs as .VII. planetes li at monstré e dit,
De quel colur eles sunt li prof escrit.
Pensive est mult la dame quant ces merveilles vit.

Les planetes del ciel es tables li enseigna,
Chascune en sa colur mult bien li devisa;   205
La colur del solail al crestal compara
La lune à l'adamant, Martem vermeil nota,
Mercure à verdor, Venerem assigna
A colur de saphir; raison de ceo mostra.
Kant la dame le sot mult par s'esmerveilla.   210
"Beau maistre," fait la dame, "e de mei que serra?
"Ja me fait l'en saveir ke quant li reis vendra

100

mule, she went back to the palace after having
played enough. The lady went to bed, and, not
having forgotten, sent for the vassal.

   He was astonished once again by her beauty.
As he sat opposite her, Olimpias told him, "I have
so much to ask you. Are you an astronomer? What
arts do you possess? Tell me where you have
learned all this." "Oh, Queen," he told her, "no
art equals you, and you know more about art than
anyone. You can tell everyone's fate, explain all
dreams, all people, all deception. Not by fate
nor by magic has my heart been ripped. By heaven
we have been blessed. By the planets' courses
have I been conquered, and no other charm do I
have to help myself, even though it is my
speciality." Olimpias said to him: "Now tell me
gentle friend, why did you stare at me today?"
"Beautiful lady," said he, "there is no one to
equal you in beauty. I remember it very well so I
will tell you why. In Egypt when I was reading
about this art, it said that in the temple a
sacrifice was made to all gods. I heard one
reason for this, and I will tell you the truth as
promised. You will advise me according to your
judgment. I was delighted to see you thus
attired."

   The lady moved towards the edge of the bed
wearing only a night-shirt and a silk dressing
robe. She wore a beautifully wrought golden
crown. Her vassal was dressed very strangely, and
though she tried to be attentive to his words, she
laughed uncontrolledly. He looked at her face and
admired it greatly. It was dangerous to speak
before this idol, but he wished to stay within
sight of her. From a golden table he read to her
and showed her the course of the seven planets and
said almost what color they were. The lady was
most attentive to these marvels.

   He showed her the planets of the sky, drawing
each very carefully in its color. He compared the
sun to crystal, the moon to a diamond, Mars to a
ruby, Mercury to greenness, Venus to the sapphire.
The lady marveled at all of this and asked

"Qu[e] il me deit guerpir, (e) altre moiller prendra."
"Kant l'oit Nectanabus le conseil esgarda,
"La lune e les planetes es signes que trova,   215
"Par lur equacium largement assuma,
"Totes les aventures qu[e] il volt esprova,
"E rent li jugement de coe qu'el(e) demanda;
"E dit: "Ke coe vus dit de riens ne vus gaba:
"Li rois guerpira vos, (e) altre moiller prendra,   220
"Mais un enfant anceis, dame, de vous naistra.
"Dieu de terre ert nomé, voz hontes vengera,
"Les regnes d'environ trestuz guvernera,
"Jusqu'au chief d'Oriant la terre conquerra,
"Si hardi ne si pruz onc arme ne porta.   225
"Amos, li diex de Libie, en vus l'engendera;
"E por icest veir dist à vus m'envei[é] a.
"Or(e) vous appareillez (anuit) e à vus aparra
"Pa[r] soigne tut iceo ke faire convendra."
La dame entent ses diz, mult [fort] li en pesa,   230
E tint le pur desvé de coe qu[e] il conta.
Dit li dunc ke ses diz a nul foer ne crerra
De ci la qu'ele veie coment (goe) estre purra.
Li maistre prent congié, à son ostel en va;
Canque mestier li fu à cel art purçhaca,   235
Les herbes acceptables [con]coilli & tribla,
Puis en après les jucs par son sen si medla,
E puis de virgine cire une ymage molla;
Le non de la reïne par lettre figura,
En un lit qu[e] ot fait cele ymage cocha,   240
Environ icel lit chandeles aluma,
Del jus qu'il ot des herbes cel' ymage arusa,
Par charmes qu'il saveit souvent la conjura.
Qanque Nectanabus à l'ymage parla
La reïne en son lit par avision songa: 245
Vis li fut que uns dragons enz en la chambre entra,
Puis vint jusq'à son lit, en home se mua,
Après li se cocha e estreit l'enbraça,
E qu[e] il l'acolout & sovent la baissa,
E q[ue] al departir, encente la laissa.   250
La dame suspira e del songe esveilla.
Nectanabus idunc ses karectes fina;
Tost e ignelement pur le vassal manda.
E quanqu'ele out veü priveement conta;
Il dist que tut est veirs icee qu'ele songa.   255
Un lit après le seon faire li comanda,
Pur estre près de li, e dit qu'il i girra,
Contre cele aventure si la confortera,
De mal e de poür par tut la deffendra.
Ele fist faire le lit si cum il le loa.   260

102

whether, when the king returned, he would leave
her. And Nectanabus answered, "This I can tell
you." She had asked if the king would leave her
and take a new wife. Nectanabus advised her that
he would find the answer for her in the signs of
the moon and the planets and warned her not to
make light of anything he said. He said, "The
king will abandon you and take another, but an
heir, Madame, will be born to you. He will be
called king of the earth and your shame will be
avenged. He will govern everything, even the
East. He will be the strongest and bravest.
Amos, the god of Lybia, will be his father, and I
have been sent to tell you this. Be ready tonight
and he will appear." The lady listened very
carefully and was troubled. She said she would
not believe it until she saw it. Nectanabus went
back to his lodging and readied the necessary
herbs and intestines and mixed them with some of
his own blood. He then molded an image from
virgin wax and printed the queen's name on it. He
placed the image on the bed and lit candles all
around it, then sprinkled the image with the blood
mixture and prayed to it with special charms. As
he spoke to the image, the queen, in her bed,
dreamed: A dragon entered her room, came to her
bed and turned into a man. He then lay beside her
and embraced her and kissed her many times. When
he left, she was with child. The lady sighed and
awoke from her dream. Nectanabus had succeeded
with his talisman. The queen quickly sent for
Nectanabus and, in private, told him of her dream.
He affirmed everything. He ordered a bed to be
placed next to hers so that he could be nearby to
help her if she needed him. He promised to defend
her against evil and fear. She carried out his
orders.

Coment Alisandre fut engendré.

Tut par le los le maistre le lit faire [li] fist,
Richeises & honnors idunc li pramist.
Qant tut fu(s)t apresté Nectanabus li dist
Que la chambre mundast contre coe qu'il venist,   265
En guise de dragun le dieu venir veïst,
Sanz noise e sanz freür en son lit le meïst,
Belement e soef illoec l'atendist
E que mot ne sona[s]t quei qu[e] ele unc oïst.
Une pel de moton ouvec les cornes prist,   270
Une coroune d'or sur les cornes assist,
En semblant de dragon l'autre part i fist
De virgine cire jointe, e puis dedens se mist,
Puis le lit a l[a] dame par tel semblant requist.

Par artimage fist tele conjunction: 275
Tresqu'al lit est venuz rampant comme dragon.
[E] la dame l'esgarde, devant le veit multon,
Ne quidout que ce fust se Amos le dieu non.
Le vassal vient al lit e ist de la tuison;
Ovec li se cocha en guise de baron.   280
Tut altretiel le sent com en la vision
L'aveit devant veü en la conjureison.
Al departir l'a dit par mult brieve raison:
"En tei ai engendré le seigneur Phelippun,
"Reis ert poest[e]ïs de mainte nation,   285
"Par force conquerra meint[e] grant region,
"De tu[s] reis terriens averat subjection."
Priveement s'en veit après icel sermon;
En son lit se couchat qu'el(e) n'eüst suspecion.
La dame lieve sus; vient à Nestanabon,   290
De quanque oï & vit [li] dit s'entention,
Tut si cum il ne sust cele subduccion;
Ele n'[ent]endeit mie en la traison.

La dame l'araisone e dist li: "Maistre cher,
Quidez [vous] qu'il ne voille à mei plus repeirer? 295
"Mielz valt l'amur de dieu que de nul chevalier.
"Je l'aim si faitement ne m'en sai conseiller.
"Il n'est pas dieu de Libie s[e] il me fait danger,
"Kar icest[e] raison qui seit dreiturer.
"Qant en peinne m'ad mise dunc me deit aleger,   300
"Venir mei conforter, ma peinne assuager."
Nectanabus li dit: "Joe [en] sui messager;
"Ensemble od vus serrai tut privé chamb[e]rer
"Qant le voudreiz aveir joe li [sar]ai nuncier;
"Dites a mei le ma(t)in, si l'auras al coucher,   305
"Si pensez del celer car (coe) vous averat mester;

104

How Alexander was conceived.

The bed for Nectanabus was readied, and honors and riches were promised to him. When all was ready, Nectanabus said that the bedroom should be armed against what was to come: the god would be disguised as a dragon which would come quietly and undetected. The queen must wait patiently and be beautiful. Nectanabus took a sheepskin with horns and placed a crown of gold upon them. He took a second part resembling a dragon and fastened the two parts with virgin wax, then crawled in and went to the queen's bed.

By his art he performed this magic act. He bounded toward the bed like a dragon. The lady saw him. She saw a sheep, yet never doubted that it was the god Amos. Nectanabus came to her bed, got out of his disguise and into bed with her. When he left he quickly told her, "In you have I engendered a king and powerful ruler of nations, who by force will conquer many powerful lands, and to whom all earthly kings will be subject." Nectanabus left after these words and went quietly to his bed without the queen's knowledge. She got up and went to tell Nectanabus what had happened as if he did not know a thing. She suspected nothing.

The lady reasoned and said: "Dear master, do you think he will not appear to me again? I value much more the love of a god than the love of a knight. I love him so I cannot console myself. He cannot be the god of Lybia if he makes me suffer. He should come and comfort me in my condition." Nectanabus told her: "I am only his messenger, but if you will be alone in your bedroom and tell me when you want him, I will give him the message. Tell me in the morning if you wish him that night, but do not change your mind

"Si haut hom[e] com dieu ne deit hom corroucer."
(N)e les clefs de sa chambre li fait [i]dunc bailler,
Q'entrer puisse e issir se (li) lui volt enveier;
Mult souvent fu prié de cee dunt dust prier.   310

La reïne engroissa, el vis fut tote teinte;
Dist a Nectanabus: "De mal sui trop ateinte;
"Li reis me fet occire s[e] il me troeve enceinte."
Nectanabus [l]i dist: "Lassiez iceste pleinte,
"Mar en aiez (ja) poour kar ne serrez ateinte;   315
"Si naist à l'enfant par naturel empeinte
"La semence de vous par le peire est seinte;
"Li reis le doutera, poür en aura meinte."

Del ostur tramis au rei Phelippe en sa avision.

Par art ad enchanté li maistre[s] un ostur
E tramet le en l'ost Phelippun son seignur,   320
La noit li fet veer en songe la verrur,
Pois si l'ad esveillé, li reis en out poür;
Ses devins et ses sages manda(s)t devant [le] jour,
Le songe q'ad veü tut [par] ordre dist lur,
Coment li dragons vint e vint ovec s'oisur;   325
Dit lur q'enceinte estoit d'un riche empereour
"Que ma mort vengera, ma peinne, ma dolur;
"Desur son umblil pris jou de verte colur.
"La meitié d'un leon forma enz en la flur,
"Orguillus chief avoit, onques ne vi greignur;   330
"La forme del soleil i fut od sa lusur.
"Le leons le feri d'un suen espié en l'ur,
"E là ù joe esteie en issi fait errur
"Un ostur m'esveilla, mult en oi grant poür
--Veirs est q'avez veü," dient si divinur,   335
"La reine est enceinte, n'en aiez pas dolur,
"Grius est qui l'engendra, coe note la verdur,
"La mei[tié] del leun signefie l'enur
"E l'orgoil que li emfes avera en la primur;
"Bon[s] reis ert e hardiz, onc em ne vit meillur, 340
"Orient conquerra par force e par vigur,
"Tant loinz cum c'em purra aler pur [la] chalur,
"Cee note le soleil où l'espié gist [de]sur;
"A ce que (vous) dites sumes verrai expositur."
Puis guerreiat li reis par force e par vigur,   345
Abati la cité, escra[van]ta la tur,
Repaire à Macedoine dreit al chief de s'onur;
Sa femme troeve enceinte, si'n ad [trop] grant hisdur
Ele dist que Amos (le dieu) l'ad mis en cel labur; 349
Plus n'en parlat li reis, mès semblant fist d'irrur.

as he is a god and will become angry." She gave
him the keys to her bedroom and told him to send
the god whenever he wanted her.

     The queen began' to grow with child. She
blushed. She said to Nectanabus: "I fear danger.
The king will have me killed if he finds me with
child." Nectanabus told her: "Do not worry. You
are wrong to be afraid for there is no reason.
The child has been engendered by holy seeds, and
if the king doubts it, it is he who should be
afraid."

**How a shortwing hawk is transmitted to Philip in a
vision.**

     Nectanabus, by his art, transmitted a vision
of a hawk to Philip in the East. At night in a
dream, he made him look out the window and see the
hawk. When Philip awoke he was frightened. He
called his wisemen and counselors before daybreak
and told them of his dream about how a dragon came
to his wife, and how his wife was with child by a
rich emperor: "May my death avenge my pain and
sorrow. Beneath his navel a green color appeared.
Half a lion was formed inside a flower. He had a
proud head. Never have I seen greater. The image
of the sun was his mane. When the lion saw me he
roared, and there where I was standing I saw a
hawk who awakened me and I was very fearful."
"Let's see what you saw," said his deviner. "The
queen is with child. Be not sad. Grius has
engendered her. That we know by the green color.
Half a lion signifies honor and the pride that the
infant will have as a child; he will be a good and
hardy king. Never will there be better. He will
conquer the Orient by his force and vigor, and
will rule as far as the sun reaches." So the king
battled by force and might, razed the city and
destroyed the tower, and left straight for
Macedonia. He found his wife with child. She
explained very calmly that it was Amos (the god)
that had put her in this state. The king no
longer spoke. He seemed vexed.

107

Coment Nectanabus se mua en dragon.

Mult est li reis irez, ne siet cui est l'emfant.
Nectanabus veit bien qu'il li fait mal semblant;
Atorne ses engins cum home decevant,
Contre le rei volt estre à la dame guarant.
Avint (que li) rei Phelippun tint une feste grant;   355
Tuit i furent si prince e si conte vaillant,
Kant il orent mangié & erent en seant,
En guise de dragon le mestre vint avant,
Parmi cel haut paleis mult fierement rampant;
Quinze teises fut bien la coe traïnant,   360
Gitat feu des narilles, hidusement siblant;
Semblant d'abatre fait les murs qui sunt estant.
Li conte e li baron de poür vont fuiant,
Si hardi bacheler od les coarz musçant,
Lur armes demanderent de poür li alquant;   365
Olimpias l'entent, il vint a li corant;
Sun chief mist en ses curs, (e) ses piez en son devant,
La reïne le maine tut entur en estant,
Quida (que) coe fut Amos, le dieu qu'ele amat tant;
Corent i chevalie[r] e corent i serjant;   370
Entour [i]cel dragon, de loinz env[i]ronnant,
Tuit se tindrent en pais, n[en] i out nul parlant,
E pur la grant merveille où il sont attendant;
Jamès n'orrez parle[r] d'un si fait truiant
Là où [tres]tout li peoples fut à lui entendant   375
En egle se mua, si s'en ala volant;
Ore est Phelippe cert dont einz esteit doutant.

De la feisante ke pont le oef al giron.

Avint puis qu[e] il fu en une region.
Et mult i aveit bestes, oissels à grant foison.
Une feisant[e] vint volant (tres)tut à bandon: 380
Un oef laissat chaïr sur les curs Phelippun.
L'oes chait, si depeça(s)t; si'n eissi un dragun;
Mult esteit petitet, si rampat environ.
Le test dunt ert eissu, pur aveir guareison
Il n'i poeit entrer ne [de] desuz n'en sum,   385
Ne contre le soleil trouver deffension;
Mort fu li dragonsels par itel achaisun.
Li reis manda(s)t un sages [qui] Antifon ot non,
Nul ne sot plus de li de la stellacion,
Priet li qu'il li die de cee s'entencion.   390
[E] cil fait tost ces sorz e sa conjunccion;
Puis, si l'espont al rei par mult chere raison:
"Del fiz vostre reïne coe est la vision:

How Nectanabus changed himself into a dragon.

The king was very angry, not knowing to whom
the child belonged. Nectanabus, seeing that he
was suspected, began to think of magic ways in
which he could get out of the situation. King
Philip threw a big feast. Everyone came, princes
and valiant counts. When they had eaten and were
still seated, Nectanabus appeared disguised as a
dragon and moved bravely around the room dragging
a tail ninety feet long behind him, breathing fire
through his nostrils and whistling hideously. It
seemed as though he would bring down the walls of
the castle. The counts and barons fled in fright.
Even the bravest of men had weak hearts. Some of
them asked for their arms. Olimpias heard this
and the dragon ran to her. He placed his head at
her heart and his paws on her lap. The queen
comforted him, thinking he was Amos, the god she
so dearly loved. Knights as well as servants ran
to help. They surrounded the dragon but kept
their distance. All held their breath. No one
spoke. And to everyone's surprise, while they
waited--never had such a story been heard--there
before them, the dragon changed into an eagle and
flew away. Now Philip was no longer in doubt
about his wife's story.

Of the pheasant which, in flight, lays an egg.

Soon after, Philip was hunting in a region
well populated with animals and birds. A pheasant
flying overhead laid an egg. The egg broke and
out of it came a dragon. It was quite small, and
it scurried about. It tried to get back into its
shell but could not. It had no defense against
the sun, which soon killed the little dragon. The
king sent for one of his wise men whose name was
Antifon--no one knew more than he about stars--and
asked him to interpret this last phenomenon.
Antifon soon wisely concluded: "Of your queen's
son here is the vision:

"Que rendra tut le monde en sa subjeccion,
"La reondesce de l'oef est l'entrepretaciun.   395
"Ceo que li dragons morust de fors sa maison,
"E jeovenes e petit, sanz consolation,
"Est, reis, à cel enfant signification,
"Joevenes e petiz conquerant morra par traison
"E fors de son païs; coe est l'exposicion.   400

Coment Alisandre nasquist & des merveilles k'avindrent quant il nasquist.

Li ventres a la dame à son terme est pris;
Necta[na]bus la lune par l'astralabe enquis
Et [si] dist à la dame: "Une rien vous devis,
"Se li emfes ore neist, povres ert & mendis,
"Coarz e recreanz, de bataille fuistis,   405
"Prison à moltes genz, pain querant e chaitis;
"Pur ceo vous tenez ore, si'n aurez los e pris.
La dame s'est tenue, tant i ont engin mis;
Revenent li assauz; ele regette cris.
Necta[na]bus li dist: "Par fei, ore est mult pis, 410
"Kar s[e] il ore naist dunc ert cochez demis,
"L'autre meité ert home de la chere, del vis;
"Tenez vous ore bien kar dès ainz vous garnis."
Par engin se rastient, si cum anceis vous dis;
E les assauz [re]venent de l'enfant qui fut vis,   415
Sa nature le volt e il fut volentis;
Grant dolur ot la dame, sis quers [en] fu pertis,
Necta[na]bus (en fu) dolent e fierement pensis;
Regarda as planetes, à l'ore fut baïs,
E dist à la reine: "Ore est tut bien assis,   420
"Laissez le tost venir, car reis ert poe[s]tis,
"Gouvernera grant terre, sire de maint païs,
"Hardiz e conquerant contre ses ennemis;
"Iceo est le veirs dist (e) que peiça vus pramis."
Atant nasqui li emfes, joie en ont ses amis.   425

Al na[i]stre de l'emfant avint grant aventure:
Toute terre crolla, mer mua sa figure,
Li soleil sa clarté, la lune sa nature;
Fist escliz e toneire e vent à desmesure;
Tenercle fut le jor com(e) coe fu[s]t nuit obscure, 430
Mult s'en espo[e]nta chascune creature,
Li peisson en la mer, bestes en lur pasture;
Hardiz fut e vaillanz qui de vivre en eust cure.
Li reis Phelippe dit e [par?] sa mere jure
Que aucune merveille ert de cele creature;   435
Pur lui est l'oscur(e)té, la pluie e la freidure,

110

He will have the whole world subject to him. The
roundness of the egg shows this. The fact that
the dragon died outside of his shell while still
young and without consolation means, my king, that
the young conqueror will die as a result of
treason and away from his country."

**How Alexander is born and of the miracles that occur at
his birth.**

The queen was now ready to deliver.
Nectanabus examined the moon through his astrolabe
and said: "One thing I must explain: if the
child is born now he will be poor, a begger, and a
coward. He will flee from battle, be put into
prison to beg for bread, and will be tortured.
Therefore you must wait a while." She waited, but
the pains began again and she screamed.
Nectanabus said: "Please. Now is even worse. If
he is born now he will be half-hog and half-man.
Be strong and wait, for you have an heir to
protect." The queen realized her responsibility
and worked hard to keep the anxious and violent
child from being born. Finally Nectanabus gave
the word: "All is favorable, give birth to your
young king who will govern great lands and be lord
of many countries." The child was born and all
rejoiced.

At the birth of the child great events
occurred: the earth quaked, the sea rose, the sun
shone brighter, and the moon changed its nature.
There was an eclipse and there was thunder and
great wind. The day turned dark as night and all
creatures were very much afraid--the fish in the
sea, the beasts in the pasture. He who wished to
go on living was truly brave. King Philip swore
by his mother that whatever these wonders might
mean for the child, for him they represented
darkness, rain, cold, and madness for as long as

E folie li semble qu[e] il tant vit & dure;
S'il vit il en ferunt mult male noreture.
Li maistres tient ses diz trestuz à demesure
E dit à la reine ke tuit en seit seüre.   440
Li tenz [s'en] est tournez e parti la leidure.
Li emfes out norice [e] sage e bien maure
Qui le norist e aprent saveir e parleure
Desi là que mis l'unt à grieve portreiture.

La mere fist l'emfant mult doucement norir;   445
Itant crut en .viii. ans que bien poet rei servir,
Dis maistres le comandet, qu'il i deit obeir;
Ke li uns li aprent sei chaucer e vestir,
E li altres (à) parler cum se deit contenir,
E le tierz chevalcher amer e eschermir,   450
E à porter ses armes e en cheval saillir,
E poindre et ateindre e traire e ferir.
E li .vii. li apernent les .vii. arz (à) retenir,
[Si] cum opposer deit e argument faillir
[E] chanter par musique, set de herbes por garir,   455
Cum deit parler en court e à trestuz plaisir,
E longur e haltur mesurer par aaimer,
E garder as esteilles, lor nons à retenir.
Assez aprent li emfes si à chief poet venir.
E quant li uns le lesse, l'altre le veit saisir;   460
D'estre oisdif ou jolif n'avoit il [nul] leisir:
A peine poet manger ou beivre ou dormir.
Que or(e) voldra bons vers oimès les poet oïr,
De veire estoire estraiz, coe oez bien garantir.
Alixandre est de ce qu'il se volt esbaldir   465
E torner à barnage e d'enfance eissir,
Pener sei de bien faire e los volt acoillir.

Unques plus bel de li ne fut emfes terestre:
Bloi peil avoit e crep, gros oil e vair le destre,
E come leonine aveit neir l'oil senestre;   470
E cresseit en barnage, à tuz plaiseit sun estre.
Bien saveit de cheval, eschermer de palestre,
De chiens e de forez, oisels jeter e pestre;
D'engin e de lettrure & de labour champestre;   474
Kar li bons (reis) Aristotles il fu sur tuz son mestre,
Icil fu le plus sage, coe sevent clerc e prestre,
[Qu]e onkes fu el mund, sanz Jesu le celestre.

**De Bucefal le cheval Alixandre, e coment Bucefal
ma[n]ga la gent.**

Avint si q'a un jor li forein mareschal
Presenterent al rei un merveillus cheval,
A force d'establie si fut pris en .i. val;   480

he lived. If the child lived he would raise him
indifferently. Nectanabus heard these words and
hastened to tell the queen that all was as
predicted. Her color and her beauty returned.
The child had a wise nurse and grew well. She
nursed him with care and taught him to be wise and
to speak.

The mother had the child so carefully trained
that he matured quickly and by age eight was able
to serve the king. He had ten teachers whom he
obeyed. One taught him to shoe and dress himself,
another how to speak and behave, a third to love
riding and dueling. He learned how to carry arms
and mount a steed, how to fight and capture and
hurl and strike. He learned about the seven arts,
how to oppose and win an argument, how to sing to
music and know healing herbs, how to speak at
court and how to please everyone, how to measure
length and height with a compass, how to follow
the stars, and to know their names. Thus the
child was taught so that he could one day be king.
When one teacher was through with him another came
and took him. He had no leisure time to himself.
He hardly had time to eat or drink or sleep. Now
he who wants to hear good verse can hear it from
now on, for I guarantee that you will witness a
strange story. Alexander was one who wished to
rejoice in knighthood and leave childhood behind.
He knew trouble and welcomed it.

Never before had there been a more beautiful
child on this earth. He had curly blond hair and
large eyes. The right eye was green, and, as if
to complement it, the left eye was black. He grew
fast and his manners pleased all. He knew horses
well and how to duel from them. He knew dogs and
forests, and how to hunt with birds and on foot.
He knew machines of war, as well as literature and
field work. Because the mighty Aristotle was his
greatest teacher, he became the wisest man known
to cleric and priest except for the heavenly Jesus.

**Of Bucephalus, Alexander's horse, and how he ate
people.**

It came to pass that one day the stable
servant presented to the king a marvelous horse in
order to determine its value. There was no one

Nul n'i out si hardi qui li donast estal.
Par chaenes de fer l'amenent li vassal;
Mult fu bel e bien fait, si semble emperial,
Mès d'une crueltér fut il trop bestial:
Il ne volleit suffrir frein ne sele à peitral,   485
Homes volleit manger plus q'estraim fr[u]mental.
L'om li dona icels qui el reigne font mal,
Qui jugé sont à mort par jugement real.
E por ceo fu nomé le cheval Bucifal
Une corroune ot el front com(e) ceo fut de roal,   490
E teste aveit de tor e jube bestial,
Fors li rois Alisandre n'i monta hom(e) mortal,
Si cum dans Sulins dit, que tant par fu leal.
En un celer le ferment desuz la tur aval
Qu'il ne face à le gent mais pecchié criminal.   495

Coment Alisandre oscist son pere, e coment Nectanabus
reprist Alixandre.

[Par] defors la cité, encoste d'une creille,
Desur l'ur d'un fossé, en travers d'une reille,
F[es]eit Nectanabus chascune nuit sa veille,
Alixandre ovec li; il l'aprent sanz chandeille
Del soleil, de la lune, conoistre meinte esteille,   500
D[es] engins e des sorz, de charmes la merveille.
Quant assez sout de l'art li vallet s'apareille,
Qu'il le voudra ocirre là ù à lui conseille:
El fossé le trebuche com(e) li maistre someille,
Mortel cop li dona amont par son l'orreille,   505
La char riés jusq'à l'os et les chevolz en peille,
Dehet [ait] tel clerjoun qui si sun mestre esveille!
Nectanabus ad dit: "A quei m'as ceo fait, sire?"
Alixandre respont: "Tut le mond seus descrire,
"E juger (de) bien e mal de chascune matire,   510
"E ne seus deviner qui tei deveit ocire;
"Des altres devinoes, de tei ne sous nient dire.
"Or(e) gis illec envers, tu n'as mestier de mire;
"Par les esteilles poet ces aventures lire,
"M'est avis endreit (de) tei q'astronomie empire.   515
"Ouan mès ne f[e]ras nul volt de virgine cire,
"Ne charme ne nul sort, ne herbes boillir ne quire.
"L'um deit l'astronomie e blasmer e despire
"Qui ne veit s'aventure & tuz les altres mire."
De icest dit ad li mestres grant deol e ire.   520

Ceo dist Nectanabus el fossé où giseit:
"Jeo savoie bien que mon fiz m'(en) ocirreit.
--Qui est dunc vostre [fiz]?" Alixandre diseit.
Dunc li ad conté ordre cum il son fiz esteit,
L'assembler & l'engin com engendré l'aveit.   525

114

that could tame him. He was led in iron chains by
the servants. He was very handsome and well
favored, imperial looking. He would not tolerate
reins or saddle and preferred men to hay. He was
given condemned men to eat, and he was thus named
Bucephalus. He had a crown on his forehead as if
he were royal, and a bull's head and a beastly
mane. Except for Alexander, no mortal man could
ride him. Just as Sulins said, and it was true
throughout the land, in cells beneath the tower,
prisoners, out of fear of being eaten, committed
only small crimes.

**How Alexander killed his father, and how
Nectanabus criticized Alexander.**

Each night outside the walls of the city atop a
high cliff, Nectanabus and Alexander kept watch.
Without even the help of a candle Nectanabus
taught Alexander about the sun and the moon, about
recognizing stars, about some tricks, about
sorcery and the marvels of magic. When Alexander
felt he knew enough of that, he prepared himself.
He wanted to kill Nectanabus right then and there.
He threw Nectanabus off the cliff while he was
sleeping. He wounded him mortally on the head,
near his ear. His flesh was torn to the bone and
his hair was pulled off the scalp. Cursed was the
young scholar when his master came to. Nectanabus
asked: "Why have you done this to me, sire?"
Alexander answered: "You were able to foretell
everyone's future except your own. You could
never have guessed that I was going to kill you."
This made Nectanabus very sad and angry.

     He said from the bottom of the cliff where he
lay: "I knew very well that my son would kill
me." "And who then is your son?" asked Alexander.
Nectanabus explained everything to him. Alexander

115

Alixandre out petié de ceo qu'il oit & veit,
Prent son pere en son col(e) s'en vait à l'ostel dreit.
Si le couche el paleis, veant sa gent, tut freit;
A sa mere le conte à un conseill estreit;
(&) ele mult s'esmerveille de ceo qu'il li conteit. 530
Ensevelir le fait(meintenant) al mielz qu'el[e] saveit.

was very sad and pitied his father and took him
straight home. He had his servants take him and
then he explained the story to his mother who was
very much surprised. The queen had Nectanabus
prepared for funeral as well as she could.

Julius Valerius' Account of the Birth of Alexander:

Text and Translation

--Edna S. deAngeli

Gower made use of at least two Latin prose sources for his tale of Alexander: the lost Nativitas et Victoria Alexandri Magni of the Archipresbyter Leo, generally called the Historia de Preliis (ca. 950 A.D.) and the Res Gestae Alexandri Macedonis of Julius Valerius (3rd or 4th century A.D.). These versions derive ultimately from a Greek source, the so-called "Pseudo-Callisthenes" or "Aesopus" but actually anonymous. The Historia de Preliis, although not extant in its original form, survived via recensions known as J^1, J^2, and J^3. The latter two were especially popular in Gower's time, circulating in the vernacular as well as in Latin. In this tradition, the Bamberg MS (abbreviated "Ba") is thought to be the closest to Leo's original Latin, and fortunately is available in an English translation by M. Schlauch (Medieval Narrative, A Book of Translations, New York, 1928). The relevant portion of Julius Valerius' Res Gestae dealing with the birth of Alexander and the role of Nectanabus, appears here in fairly literal translation. By comparing the two, the student of Gower can see how the English poet played his Latin sources off against each other. The text of Valerius is taken from the Teubner text, ed. Bernard Kuebler, Iuli Valeri Alexandri Polemi Res Gestae Alexandri Macedonis Translatae ex Aesopo Graeco, Leipzig 1888. Kuebler's excellent apparatus criticus has been deleted as being extraneous to the focus of this source book. Latin scholars interested will find in the apparatus all variant manuscript readings, including those in the Zacher epitome, as well as references to major nineteenth-century editions.

119

LIBER PRIMUS

QUI EST

ORTUS ALEXANDRI

---

1. Aegyptii sapientes sati genere divino primi feruntur permensique sunt terram ingenii pervicacia et ambitum coeli stellarum numero assecuti. Quorum omnium Nectanabus prudentissimus fuisse comprobatur, quippe qui quod alii armis, ille ore potuisse convincitur. Denique mundialia elementa ei parebant, adeo ut, si metus bellicus illi immineret, non exercitum, non machinamenta martia moveret: quin potius ingressus aulae penita regiaeque secreta ibi se solitarium abdebat invecta secum pelvi. Quam dum ex fonte liquidissimo impleret, ex cera imitabatur navigii similitudinem effigiesque hominum illic collocabat. Quae omnia cum supernare coepissent, mox moveri ac vivere visebantur. Adhibebat etiam et virgulam ex ligno ebeni et praecantamina loquebatur, quibus vocaret deos superos inferosque, sicque laborabat pelvi naviculam submergi. Ex quo fiebat, ut simul cum submersione illius cerae et cereis insessoribus etiam omnes hostes, si qui adesse praenuntiabantur, pelago mergerentur. Itaque multo tempore regno ac securitate potitus est. Quodam igitur tempore nuntiatum est ei multas adversus eum gentes una conspiratione atque eadem voluntate consurrexisse, scilicet Indos, Arabes Phoenicesque, Parthos et Assyrios, nec non et Scythas, Alanos, Oxydracontas, Seres atque Caucones, Hiberos, Agriophages, Eunomites et quaecunque sunt orientis barbarae gentes. Quibus ille auditis plausum dans manibus magno risu dissolutus est.

BOOK ONE

THE BIRTH OF ALEXANDER

Epitome. 1. Egyptian wise men are said to have been born of divine stock and the first to measure the earth and number the stellar orbits. Of all these Nectanabus was proved to have been the wisest, since he could accomplish with words what others did by force of arms. Finally, worldly elements were prepared for him in such a way that, when fear of war hung over him, he would go deep into the recesses of his royal palace, all alone, and take a basin with him. While he was filling this with pure spring-water, out of wax he would fashion a likeness of a boat and put in it human images. When all these things began to float, soon they appeared to be in motion and to live. He also used an ebony wand and spoke incantations by which he called on gods above and below, and so he contrived to have the boat submerged in the basin. As a result it would happen that all his actual enemies would be submerged in the sea along with the sinking of the wax figures. And so for a long time he was secure in power over his kingdom. Then a report reached him that a huge conspiracy was stirred up against him, including Indians, Arabs, Phoenicians, Parthians, Assyrians, not to mention Scythians, Alani, Oxydracontae, Seres, as well as Caucones, Hiberi, Agriophagi, Eunometae, and all other barbaric peoples of the east. After he heard about this, he clapped his hands and laughed aloud.

121

2. Igitur ad consuetam artis confugit peritiam et more solito adhibuit sibi pelvem atque omnia alia instrumenta. Quibus intellexit se vincendum atque ab hostibus capiendum, nisi fugae consuleret. Mox autem raso capite et barba collectisque omnibus quae sibi erant pretiosarum opum, adpulit Macedoniae. Ibique amictus veste linea, astrologum se professus, vim peritiae suae cum magna admiratione commendabat.

Ergo iam longe celebratior apud Macedones Nectanabus erat, ut fama eius ne Olympiadam quidem reginam lateret. Coepitque consulere peritiam viri absente tunc coniuge. Nam Philippus bello forte tunc aberat. Igitur ingredi iussus vel ad primam Olympiadis visionem miratione formae eius Nectanabus ita motus est, ut amori mulieris dederetur, quod eum ferme ex corporis intemperie facile erat his voluptatibus vinci. Ingressus tamen protenta manu reginam havere iubet, non dominae eam appellatione dignatus, qui se olim dominum fuisse meminisset. Resalutato igitur ac sedere iusso 'Tune,' inquit, 'ille es Nectanabus matheseos sciens? Nam quisque te consuluerit, veridicentiae tuae non refragatur. Dic ergo, quanam usus peritia adeo veri amicus cluis.' Ad id respondit: 'Multifida quidem est, o regina, ista haec nostra vaticinandi scientia, neque est in tempore omnium meminisse. Nam et interpretes somniorum et astrici, quibus omnis divinandi ratio reseratur, et multa sunt praeter haec nomina, quibus uti ad praescientiam solemus.'

3. His dictis cum acrius in vultum reginae intueretur, Olympias refert: 'Quid ita defigeris, o propheta, ubi iam me intueris?' At ille: 'Recordor enim nunc demum oraculi eius, quod apud Aegyptum a diis acceperam, oportere me reginae vera praedicere percunctanti. Quare consule super cupitis.' Et cum verbis tabulas promit, quas peritiae huiusce docti pinacam nominaverunt, opus adeo fabre absolutum, ut artifex manus certasse putaretur cum bino eloquentiae testimonio. Auro enim et ebore variatum pretium sui cum operis admiratione contendarat. Tum promit etiam septem quas rogaret stellas et horoscopum pariter, quibus singulis sui metalli species erat. Iovem enim viseres aereo lapide nuncupatum, Solem crystallo, Lunam adamante, Martem dici sub lapide ematite; sed Mercurius ex smaragdo fuit,

2. Therefore he resorted to his accustomed magic
and employed the basin and his other instruments in the
usual way. From these devices, he learned that he
would be conquered and captured by the enemy unless he
took to flight. So without delay he shaved his head
and beard, gathered up all his valuables, and set out
for Macedonia. Once there, garbed in linen, he
declared himself an astrologer and was soon renowned
for his skill.

Therefore, it was not long before Nectanabus became
so renowned with the Macedonians that his fame reached
even to Olympias the queen. And she began consulting
his magic skill, her husband being away at this time.
For as it happened Philip was away fighting a war. So,
Nectanabus was ordered to approach the queen, and, when
he saw her for the first time, he was so stirred with
admiration for her beauty that he surrendered himself
to love for her, since he was quite susceptible to
these delights of the flesh. Approaching her, he
extended his hand and compelled the queen to desire
him, not deigning to call her by her title (domina),
since he remembered that he had been a lord (dominus)
at one time. Therefore, after greeting him and
ordering him to be seated, she said, "Are you that
Nectanabus who has knowledge of mathematics? For no
matter who consults you, there is no one to oppose your
veracity. Tell me, then, what skill you use so that
you are called friend of the truth." To this he
replied, "this our knowledge of prophecy, O queen, has
many ramifications, and it is not possible to recall
all of them at one time. For there are both
interpreters of dreams and astrologers, to whom the
complete theory of divination is disclosed, and in
addition many other branches which we customarily use
for prognosticating."

3. Since he was staring at the queen rather
intently as he said this, Olympias replied, "Why such a
fixed stare, O prophet, when you look at me?" And he
in reply, "Because at last I remember that oracle which
I had received from the gods in Egypt, that I should
make true prophecies to a queen at her request.
Therefore ask me what you wish." And with these words
he held out tablets which those men learned in this
kind of knowledge called pinaces (tablets for
painting), so skillfully worked that an artist's hand
would be thought of as double testimony for the power
to speak. For the value of the gold and ivory would
have equal claim on admiration for the work. Then he
held out seven stars and a horoscope in which there was

123

Venus vero sapphiria, Saturnus in ophite, tum
horoscopus lygdinus. Exinde mirans Olympias pinacis
illius opulentiam stellarumque mirabilem varietatem
propter sessitans iubet omne facessere famulitium, qui
aderant sibi ex ministerio regali, ut arcanum sermonem
tuto committeret, et ait: 'O tu, quaeso, intuere meam
et Philippi congruentiam; nam multa fama est, quod, si
adfuerit ex hostico, abiecta me velit in alteram
transiugari.' Ad haec ille: 'Quin ergo deprome vel
tuam vel Philippi genituram.' Quod cum illa fecisset,
Nectanabus statim suam quoque adhibet constellationem
exploraturus, an illa cum Olympiadis genitura
conveniret voluntatisque potiretur. Quod cum fore
deprehendisset, hinc orsus est: 'Non vana,' inquit,
'ista ad te fama pervenit, sed enim vera est. Ego
tamen ac si prophetes ex Aegypto opitulabor, ut queam,
ne quid de divortio formidaveris. Quod etsi foret,
vindex facto non deesset.' 'Quanam,' inquit Olympias,
'id facultate?' 'Quod enim,' Nectanabus refert,
'fatale tibi est secundum hanc, quam video, genituram
misceri deo eque isto gravidam filium nutricaturam
ultorem omnium, si quae in te Philippus audebit.' Tum
illa: 'Et cuinam,' inquit, 'deo ad torum debeor?'
Respondit: 'Ammoni Libyco. Is autem est fluvius.' De
aetate, qua visitur, quaerit. Iuvenem esse renuntiat.
De facie sciscitatur et cultu. Canum caesarie dicit et
ore praelepidum, temporibus tamen atque fronte arietis
cornibus asperatum. 'Quare,' inquit, 'paraveris te,
velut feminis mos est et reginae decorum est, ad
huiuscemodi nuptias. Videbis enim et somnium et in
somnio nuptias tibi futuras esse cum deo.' Ad haec
illa: 'Ego,' inquit, 'somnium si somniabo, non iam te
ut mago utar, enimvero dei honore venerabor.'

    4. Progressus inde Nectanabus neque oppertus in
tempus longum herbas ex scientia quaerit ad somniorum
imperia necessarias. Quibus carptis atque in sucum
pressis effigiat ex cera corpusculum feminae eique
nomen reginae cum adscripsisset, lectulum eidem
fabricatur, cui illa effigies supraponitur iuxtaque
lucernis incensis sucum herbarum potentium superfundit

an example of each metal. For you could see Jupiter's name in gold, the Sun in crystal, the Moon in diamonds, Mars in ematite stone; but Mercury was worked in emeralds, Venus in sapphires, Saturn in snake-stone, and the horoscope itself in white Parian marble. Then Olympias, marveling at the opulence of that pinace and the fabulous variety of the stars, ordered all the servants to withdraw, so she could safely have secret converse with him, and said, "I beg you, look upon my relationship with Philip; for there is much gossip that, when he comes back from enemy territory, he will cast me aside and marry another woman."

To this he replied: "First tell me your birth sign, yours and Philip's." When she had done this, Nectanabus immediately turned to the constellation to ascertain whether it would be in harmony with the birth sign of Olympias and have power over her wish. When he had figured this out, he began as follows: "That was no idle rumor that came to your ears, but in fact a true report. Nevertheless, I, a soothsayer from Egypt, will aid you as much as I can, so you need have no fear of divorce. But even if it would happen, an avenger would not be lacking to you." Olympias said, "Through what means?" Nectanabus replied, "It is decreed for you, according to the birth-sign which I see, that you have carnal intercourse with a god and that the son you will bear as a result will be your avenger in case Philip dares to do anything against you." Then she said, "And by what god am I to be seduced?" He replied, "Ammon of Libya. He is a river, you know." She asked about the age of her (future) visitor. He reported that he was a young man. She asked about his looks and appearance. He said he had a beautiful white head of hair and a very attractive face, but that his forehead and temples were roughened with ram's horns. "Therefore," he said, "you should prepare yourself, as is proper for a woman and a queen, for nuptials of this kind. For you will have a dream and in that dream you will see that you will have a marriage with a god." To this she replied, "If I really do have that dream, I shall no longer employ you as a magician, but rather I shall venerate you as a god."

4. Nectanabus then, without waiting long, sought for herbs which he knew were essential for dream control. After he had plucked them and squeezed out the juice, he fashioned out of wax a little figure of a woman; when he had inscribed the queen's name on it, he fashioned a little bed on which the little figure was placed. Lighting oil-lamps next to it, he poured

carmenque dicit efficax et secretum quo effectum est,
ut quidquid ille simulamini cereo loquebatur, id omne
fieri sibi regina sit opinata per somnium. Videt enim
se in complexibus dei, quos fore cum Ammone dixerat,
postque compleus deum sibi loquentem audierat, factam
se et utero gravem et edituram vindicem filium. Surgit
ergo de lectulo et admirata somnii maiestatem hominem
ad sese vocat et 'Ecce,' inquit, 'promissum somnium
vidi. Nam et deus erat et agebat mecum nuptiae
secretum. Igitur curam quaeso suscipias, quando id
effectum compleatur quandoque me deus iste dignetur, ut
ego quoque iugalibus me et sponso iam praeparem.' Ad
haec Nectanabus: 'Hoc quidem,' inquit, 'o domina, quod
vidisti, verum est somnium. Aderit tamen ipse etiam ad
te deus. Sed censeo mihi secessum istic iuxta tuum
cubiculum dari, ut iuste procurem, ne quis tibi metus
sit sub adventu huius numinis.'

Probat id promissi regina et vicinum cubiculo suo
secessum mago tribuit et 'Si,' inquit, 'harumce
nuptiarum cepero experimentum conceptuque sim potita,
honor regalis tibi a regina non deerit, inque te patris
adfectum fore mihi iam spes promittit.' Tum addidit
ille: 'Praecursor tibi,' inquit, 'dei mox aderit. Nam
sedenti superveniet draco clementius reptabundus. Enim
tu eo viso omnis, qui adsint, abire iubeto de medio,
nec tamen quaecunque aderunt exstinxeris lumina, sed
cum te lectulo conlocaris, opertum quidem vultum ad
verecundiam texeris velamine, tamen limis explora
vultus illos, quos iam somno praevidisti, ut si is
erit.'

Insequenti igitur die et locus mago destinatur et
ille quaevis ex arte opportuna providit, vellus
scilicet arietis quam mollissimum una cum cornibus
sceptrumque et amictum admodum candidum. Quo
superiecto efficit scientia draconem sibi veluti
mansuetum et innoxie gradientem vesperaque adventantem
cum facit ut praecursorem. Et is intrat ad feminam.
Quo viso illa mox horridula prae metu disicit quosque
praesentes, ipsa vero secundum monitum dat sese lectulo
et obnupta vultu solo oculo ad superventum opinati dei
curiose intendebat viditque illum, quem somno ante
praeceperat. At ille sceptro deposito conscensoque
lectulo nuptias agit eximque utero eius superiecta
manu, 'Habes,' inquit, 'o mulier ex nobis haec invicta
et insubiugabilia foedera. Quippe gaudeto te gravidam

126

over it the juice of the powerful herbs and chanted a strong, secret chant. All this the queen was to believe through a dream. For she saw herself in a god's embrace, which the magician had said would be Ammon, and after the embrace she heard the god speaking to her saying that he would impregnate her and she would bear a son as her avenger. Then she got up from bed, and, wondering at the grandeur of the dream, called the man to her and said, "Look, I have seen the dream you promised. For there was a god and he consummated a secret marriage with me. Therefore I beg you to consider when this will actually come to pass, when that god of yours will honor me, so that I can prepare myself for the nuptial act." To this Nectanabus said, "O mistress, what you saw was a true dream. Nevertheless the god himself will also visit you. But I think you should give me a private chamber next to yours, so that I can take care of this matter properly, lest you have any fear of the divine approach."

The queen agreed to do this and assigned him a room next to her bedroom and said, "If I have experienced these nuptials and if I conceive, you will lack no royal honor from the queen, and I should expect to feel towards you as I would to a father."

Then he added, "Soon the god's forerunner will appear to you. For there will come upon you unexpectedly when you are seated a kind, gentle creeping snake-dragon. Now, when you see it, order everyone present to go away; nevertheless do not extinguish the lamps, but when you get into bed, keep your face covered with a veil. However, out of the corner of your eye examine his appearance to see if it is the same one you saw in your dream."

So on the following day a place was assigned to the magician and he provided every sort of magic for the occasion, without doubt the fleece of a ram, as soft as possible, along with horns and a sceptre and a completely white cloak. By throwing the cloak over this, his skill produced a snake-dragon that walked gently and harmlessly, and toward evening had the snake-dragon come as the precursor (of the god).

And he walked in to the woman. At seeing him she fearfully dismissed her attendants, and she herself, following his advice, went to her bedroom and veiled her face except for one eye, and she saw that one whom she had perceived before in her dream. But he, putting

127

ex filio, quo vindice et universi orbis domino
laetare.' His ita dictis sceptroque recepto conclave
exit. Sed mane iam luciscente mulier alacrior laetitia
ut potita dei cubiculum Nectanabi inrumpit. Is e somno
excitatus ut nescius rei causam quaerit adventus. Tum
illa 'Facta,' inquit, 'sunt omnia, quae promiseras.'
Et ille sese gaudere professus est. Rursus mulier
'Ergone,' inquit, 'ultra adesse dignabitur? Nam est
mihi etiam amor ad nuptias tales. Id enim mihi sensus
coniux coniugi dedit. Nunc tamen metuo, ut ista
cessaverint.' Tum magus gaudens, quod amorem sui
mulier testaretur in hoc verbo, ait ad reginam:
'Huiusce dei minister ego sum, et cum voles talis
mariti conventum, secretum quoque praesta sollemne
mihique dicito, ut purgatione sacricula procurem, quo
ad te rursus adveniat.' Tum ergo illa deversorium
solitum Nectanabo promittit et claves cubiculi mago
dari iubet; ex quo promptior illis erat in id, quod
cupiverant, commeatus, sub opinione tamen Ammonis dei.

Sed iam alvo et lateribus excrescentibus 'Quidnam,'
inquit, 'o propheta, mihi fiet, quidve nunc opus facto
est, si adveniens Philippus cum isto me onere
deprehendat?' 'Ne metueris,' ille respondit,
'opitulabitur enim Ammon ei vitio, quod suasit, eumque
per somnium super facto docebit, ne quid tibi iste
succenseat, quod sciat deos omnium potentes esse.' In
hunc igitur modum Olympias magicis artibus ducebatur.

Sed Nectanabus sibi sacrum accipitrem parat eumque
secretius monet ire ad Philippum et loqui, quae ipse
mandaverat. Pergitque ire ales, ut iussum est, per
terras et mare Philippumque per noctem adsistens
mandatis opinionibus complet. Quippe territus somnio
evocatoque rex somniorum interprete sic ait: 'Vidi,'
inquit, 'per quietem deum quendam, facie formosum et
canitie caesariatum capitis et genae, arietis tamen
cornibus insignitum, supervenisse Olympiadi coniugi
meae seque illi nuptiis miscuisse.' Quibus patratis
haec etiam verba addiderat: 'Excepisti,' inquit, 'o
mulier, marem filium, qui adserat te et patris ultor

down his sceptre and climbing into the bed, consummated the marriage and then, putting his hand on her belly, said, "Woman, you have received from us an imperishable bond. Rejoice that you are pregnant with a son, a protector and lord of the earth in whom you will be happy." With these words, picking up his sceptre, he went out of the chamber.

In the morning when it grew light, the woman, bright with joy as one in the power of the god, broke into Nectanabus' bedroom. He, aroused from sleep, acted as though he were unaware of the reason for the queen's coming. So she said, "All that you promised has taken place." And he professed sudden rejoicing. Again, the woman said, "Will I be honored again in this way? For I really like this kind of marriage. You see, this has given me the feelings of a wife for a husband. Now I am afraid that this will come to an end."

Then the sorcerer, rejoicing that the woman bore witness in this statement that she was in love with him, said to the queen, "I am the attendant of this god, so when you want to mingle with your husband in this way, be sure to tell me secretly every time, so that I can arrange for the sacred rites of purification, by means of which he will come to you again." Then she promised Nectanabus his customary lodging and ordered the keys of her bedroom to be given to him; as a consequence he was somewhat quicker in arranging the meetings they both desired, with the sorcerer of course in the guise of the god Ammon.

But when she grew great with child, she said, "O prophet, what will happen to me, what do we need to do now in case Philip comes home and catches me with this burden?" "Don't be afraid," he replied, "for Ammon will help you out of the immorality which he urged on you; Ammon will show Philip through a dream how this happened, so that he won't be angry at you in any way, since he knows the gods are omnipotent." In this fashion, therefore, Olympias was seduced through magic.

Well, Nectanabus got himself a sacred hawk, and secretly instructed it to go to Philip and tell him what he had ordered. And the bird, as directed, started on its way through land and sea and appearing to Philip at night gave him the mandated message. Terrified by the dream, the king summoned his interpreter of dreams and spoke thus: "In my sleep I saw a god, of handsome appearance and with a fine head

129

esse laudetur.' Tum mulieris virginal biblo contegere
consignareque annulo aureo visebatur, cui inscalptio
erat solis effigies et leonis caput hastili subiecto.
Quae cum vidissem, accipiter superveniens excitare me
pulsu videbatur alarum. Quid igitur istud est, quod
portenditur?'

   Tum interpres: 'O Philippe, verum istud est nec in
aliud interpretandum, ut adsolet, opinabile. Quod enim
signari vidisti virginal feminae, fidem rei visae
testatur. Consignatio enim fides est atque veritas, ex
quo praenosti, quod illa conceperit; nemo enim vas
vacuum consignaverit. Et haec biblo, quippe cum biblus
ista vel carta nullibi gentium nisi in nostra tellure
gignatur. Aegyptium igitur semen est, qui conceptus
est, non tamen humile, sed clarum plane vel regium
propter aurei annuli visionem. Hoc enim metallo nihil
scimus esse pretiosius, in quo etiam deorum effigies
veneramur. Sed quoniam signaculum [quod] solis forma
visebatur subterque leonis caput hastile quoque
adiacens erat, is ipse, quisque nascetur, in orientis
usque veniet praepotentia possessionem, omnia audens,
quae natura est leonis, idque vi et hasta faciet, quae
una vidisti. Enimvero quoniam deum capite arietino
testaris eundemque canum, est deus Libyae Ammonis
nomine.'

   Hanc interpretationem interpretis tunc non aequo
satis animo Philippus accepit, quod homine concepisse
mulierem credidisset. Festinata igitur re bellica
Macedoniam ad suam repedat. Quo reditu mulier audito
trepidatior erat, solatiis tamen eius Nectanabus
adsidebat. Tandem igitur adveniens Philippus ut
ingressus est, reginam, cum diffidentius sibi occursare
coniugem intueretur, astu dissimulans indignationem in
haec verba solatus est: 'Me quidem clam res gesta non
est libensque te veniam impertio, quippe culpa tibi non
adhaerente, sicuti praescivi de sompnio defensante,
quod factum est, ab omni culpa, qua adlini posses.
Regibus quoque sicuti in alios vis est, ad deos tamen
potentia frixerit. Neque enim te scio popularis
alicuius amori servisse, enimvero dei deorum
pulcherrimi.' His dictis animum mulieris
instauraverat. Agit ergo gratias uxor veniae eique,
qui sibi spem eius pollicitus videbatur, prophetae
Nectanabo.

of white hair, but marked with ram's horns; this god
had come to my wife Olympias and mingled with her in
wedlock. After this, the god added the following
words, 'Woman, you have conceived a male child who will
protect you and be praised as his father's avenger.'
Then he seemed to touch the woman's womb and affix
thereon a seal with a gold signet ring on which was
engraved an image of the sun and a lion's head with a
spear beneath it. When I saw this, a sudden rush of
fear came over me. What is this, what does it
portend?"

Then the interpreter spoke: "O Philip, that dream
of yours is true, and not to be considered conjectural
in the usual way. For the fact that you saw the
woman's womb sealed is testimony to the validity of the
vision. For the signet ring seal is faith and truth,
from which you got foreknowledge that she has
conceived; nobody seals an empty vessel. And surely
these things in the book occur in the records of no
other people except those in our country. Therefore it
is an Egyptian seed which was conceived, not a lowly
one but a famous and royal one because of the vision of
the gold signet ring. For we know of no metal more
precious than this, out of which the god's images are
made. But since the seal seemed to be in the form of
the sun with the lion's head and spear below it, that
one who is to be born will come into possession of the
east with full powers; he will dare all things, like a
lion; he will act by power of the spear which you saw.
Furthermore, since you claim the god had white hair and
ram's horns on his head, that must be the god Ammon of
Libya."

At this time Philip was not quite satisfied with
the interpreter's explanation, since he believed that
it was a man who had got his wife pregnant. Therefore
quickly finishing up the war, he hurried back to his
own kingdom in Macedonia. On hearing of his return,
his wife was in a state of some alarm, but Nectanabus
tried to calm her fears.

When Philip finally arrived and entered the palace,
as he saw the queen was looking at him with some
diffidence, cleverly concealing his anger he soothed
her fears in these words: "This was not kept a secret
from me and I grant you pardon freely, since surely
there is no blame adhering to you, as I was informed in
advance in a dream absolving you of all blame.
Although kings have power over other men, their power
stops at the gods. For I know that you would not have

131

Igitur agebat interim Philippus cum muliere
coniugaliter. Nectanabus vero praesens quidem, sed
invisitatus una agebat; neque enim videri se ex arte
magica concesserat. Denique et interfuit aliquando
effervescenti iam Philippo et coniugem increpanti, quod
ille conceptus non ex deo mulieri foret. Quod cum
auribus Nectanabus usurpasset conviviumque celebre et
regium pararetur ob reversionem scilicet Philippi votum
ac redditum, omnium erat visere dapsilem satis
diffusamque lasciviam, nec tamen Philippum frontem in
laetitiam explicasse, quod praegnantem Olympiadam
admodum suspectaret. Ergo ut iam tempus convivandi
erat, statim se reficit Nectanabus et reformat in illum
draconis quidem, sed auctiorem aliquantulum tractum
eoque reptabundus triclinium penetrat, tum spectabilis
specie, tum maiestate corporis totius, tum etiam
acumine sibilorum adeo terribili et divino, ut
fundamenta etiam parietesque conclavis quati ac motari
viderentur. Ceteris igitur prosultantibus ac
delabentibus metu, una Olympias, quo fidem faceret
divino commercio, manum protendit ad bestiam. At vero
draco, ut lubentiam sui proderet, et caput in sinum
mulieris extendit et omne agmen in spiram mansuetius
colligit et genibus sinuque mulieris insidens promptum
os porrigit et cum bisulco linguae vibratu osculum
uxoris adfectat, ne quid omnino coniugali fidei deesset
apud eum maritum, cui talis visio proderetur. Hic
Philippus una metu unaque admiratione discedit. Sed
ultra Nectanabus inspiciens draconem vertit in aquilam
et volatu facessit e medio. Tunc ex admiratione
sobrius Philippus: 'O coniux', ait, 'patuit vero
argumento divini circa te numinis cultus. Vidimus enim
deum auxiliantem tibi periclitanti, quamvis quis is sit
nesciam, quippe vel Iovem credas ex aquila vel Ammonem
ex dracone.' Ad haec mulier: 'Ammonem se quidem
professus est, dum primum mecum convenire dignatus,
est, scilicet Libyae dominum universae.'

5. Enimvero pavens cum in quadam regiae parte
Philippus sessitaret, in qua aves plurimae
circumerrarent, isque intentus rebus agendis animum
occupavisset, repente gallina supersiliens eius in
sinum considensque enixa est ovum. Sed ovum illud
evolutum sinu eius humi concrepat, cuiusque testula
dissultante dracunculus, ut pote tantilli conclavis
pertenuis, egredi visitur, isque saepe circumcursans et

submitted to any human lover, but only to the
handsomest of gods." With these words he restored his
wife's equanimity. So she gave him thanks for the
pardon which the prophet Nectanabus had foretold.

Therefore, for the time being, Philip lived in
conjugal fashion with his wife. Nectanabus, to be
sure, was still present, but he kept himself invisible
by means of his magic. Eventually Philip did begin to
break out in reproach against his wife, on the ground
that he had been taken in by a woman, not by a god.
Now Nectanabus had heard that a royal banquet was to be
prepared in fulfillment of Philip's vow for safe
return; it was to be a lavish and delightful affair
for all to see, but in the midst of the festivities
Philip would reveal the fact that he suspected
Olympias' pregnancy. Therefore, when the time came for
the banquet, at once Nectanabus remade his shape and
took on the form of a dragon, but somewhat larger than
before, and creeping along in this shape he entered the
dining-hall, so striking in appearance, so majestic in
his entire physique, with such fearsome, divinely
piercing hisses, that the foundations and the walls of
the building seemed to shake and shudder. While the
others were running away or falling down in their fear,
Olympias alone, trusting in her compact with the
divinity, extended her hand to the monster. The
dragon, indeed, for his own pleasure, put his head in
the woman's lap, coiled his entire length gently around
the woman's legs and body, reached up to her mouth, and
kissed her with his forked tongue, lest any aspect of
their conjugal relationship be lacking in her husband's
presence, since it was for his sake the vision was
produced. At this point Philip was torn between fear
and wonderment. Then Nectanabus went further and
changed the dragon to an eagle and flew out of their
midst.

Then, grave with wonder, Philip said: "O wife,
clearly there is a divine power at work around you.
For we saw the god helping you and testing you,
although what god this is I do not know. Perhaps you
might believe it to be Jupiter from the eagle or else
Ammon from the dragon." To this his wife replied: "He
admitted he was Ammon, when he first deigned to come to
me, Ammon the lord of all of Libya."

5. Now when Philip, still fearful, was sitting in
a part of the palace where many birds were flying
around, and he was concentrating on things that needed
doing, suddenly a hen flew up into his lap and laid an

133

ambiens ovi testulam velle se rursus eo, unde
emerserat, condere; sed priusquam cupitum ageret,
morte praeventus est. Ea visio non parvum scrupulum
Philippo in animum iniecerat. Rex denique Antiphontem,
qui coniector id temporis egregius habebatur, arcessiri
iubet eique aperit rem visitatam: gallinam, ovum,
dracunculum, circuitum, mortem dracunculi. Sed enim
Antipho ad incrementum peritiae suae dei adminiculo
inspiratus infit regem docere: filium mox ei fore, qui
omnem mundum obiret omnemque suae dicioni subiugaret;
hunc post ambitum mundani laboris, domum iam se
vertentem, occasu celeri periturum. 'Draco quippe,'
ait, 'est regale animal. Ovum vero forma mundialis
est.' Ex quo cum draco erupisse videatur, post omnem
rotunditatis illius ambitum circuisse atque ingredi eo,
unde ortum habuerat, cupivisse, prius quidem mortuum,
quam id fieri proveniret, cuncta haec, quae praedicta
sunt, portendisse. Et his quidem in hunc modum
interpretamenti sui fidem fecerat apud Philippum.

6. Adpetente autem iam partitundinis tempore
consederat Olympias oneri partus levando. Sed
adsistens Nectanabus inspectansque coelites cursus,
notans etiam mundana secreta, peritia auctore 'Mane,'
inquit, 'quaeso, mi mulier, et vim partitudinis vince
reprimens geniturae necessitatem imminentis; quippe si
nunc fiat editus partus, servile quiddam captivumque
potentum natum iri astra minitantur.' Atque cum
obdurasset mulier obfirmatius secundisque aculeis
pulsaretur, rursus admonetur: 'Nunc etiam, quaeso,
duraveris paululum, quippe si editu victa sis, gallus
et semivir erit, qui nascetur.' Talia et blandius
loquebatur et adtrectare secretius mulierem non
differebat, tactu etiam opitulaturus att de . . .
pueri. Ac tum demum acrius intuens cursus astrorum
motusque elementorum cognoscit iam omnem mundum vim
suam in summo culmine conversionis lene librasse
solemque ipsum mediam caeli plagam et convexi celsiora
percurrere. Tunc ergo ad mulierem sic ait: 'En tempus
est,' inquit, 'voce nunc fortiore opus est et
obfirmatiore conatu, quippe quod nunc erit editum,
mundi totius dominio celebrabitur.' His femina
incitata mugitu omni vehementius ingemiscens exegit
puerum, qui ubi ad humum lapsus est, motus protinus
terrae insequitur et tonitruum crepor ventorumque

egg there. But the egg rolled off his lap and cracked on the ground; out of the shell leapt a little dragon, as though eager to emerge from such a small enclosure, then ran around the egg shell as though wanting to get back there. But before it could accomplish this, it was prevented by death. This vision threw Philip into considerable anxiety. Finally the king ordered Antiphon, who was considered the best interpreter of that time, summoned; and he told him the whole story: the hen, the egg, the baby dragon, the running around, the death.

Now Antiphon, through divine ministration, was inspired with an increase of skill to explain to the king that he would soon have a son who would traverse the whole world and subjugate it to his sway, and that after the course of his work in the outside world he would return to his home and shortly die. "The dragon," he said, "is a royal creature, whereas the egg symbolizes the world." Therefore the dragon appears to have broken out (of the shell) and to have made the whole circuit of its circumference, also to be eager to go back to that place from which it had sprung, but it died before this could be accomplished, and to have foretold all that was predicted. This interpretation served to strengthen Philip's belief in the vision.

6. Then the time was at hand for Olympias to be relieved of her burden. Nectanabus inspected the constellations, making note of secret things, and said, "I beg you, my wife, hold back and repress the impulse you feel for imminent delivery; because, if you were to give birth now, there is a warning from the stars that your son will become a slave and a captive."

Accordingly the woman held back firmly, but when she was stricken with pains a second time, again she was admonished: "Now also, I beg you, endure a while longer, for if you deliver now, your son will be a eunuch, a half-man." Then, finally, looking intently at the stars and their motion, he learned that the entire world would be under the sway of the one born at the peak of the turning of Leo and that the sun itself was traversing the central region of the sky. Then he spoke as follows to his wife: "Now the time is at hand, there is need for a stronger cry and a more vigorous effort, since the one who will be born at this time will be famous for dominion over the whole world."

Roused by these words, the woman, groaning and moaning violently, gave birth to the boy and, when he

135

conflictus, tum etiam fulgurum coruscatio, prosus ut
viseres omni mundo curam cum illa partitudine
elaboratam. Ergo ait et Philippus post solatia
gratulatoria: 'Equidem mihi fuisse, o mulier,
consilium profitebor non nutriendi, quod natum est,
propterea quod id de meo semine non provenerit; sed
enim cum videam subolem esse divinam editionemque ipsam
elementis et diis pariter cordi fuisse, votis
educationis accedo; inque memoriam eius filii, qui
mihi occubuit de prioribus nuptiis, Alexandri eidem
nomen dabo.'

7. Post vero regalius et competentius alebatur.
Nam et coronalia obsequia eidem undique confluebant tum
Macedonia tum Pella tum Thracia multigenisque aliis
gentibus in id certantibus. Atque in his exegit spatia
lactandi. Vultu formaque omni alienus a Philippo, ne
matri quidem ad similitudinem congruus, ei quoque,
cuius e semine credebatur, facie diversus, sed suo modo
et filo pulcherrimus, subcrispa paululum et flavente
caesarie, ut comae sunt leoninae, oculis egregii
decoris, altero admodum nigra quasi pupilla est, laevo
vero glauca atque coeli similis, profususque omni
spiritu et impetu, quo leones, ut palam viseres, quid
de illo puero natura promitteret. Crescebat ergo ut
corporis gratia ita studiorum quoque et prudentiae
maiestate et cum his una regiae disciplinae. Eius
nutrix Alacrinis erat, paedagogus atque nutritor nomine
Leonides, litteraturae Polynicus magister, musices
Alcippus Lemnius, geometriae Menecles Peloponnesius,
oratoriae Anaximenes Aristocli Lampsacenus,
philosophiae autem Aristoteles ille Milesius.

Enim de Mileto loqui hic longa res est et
propositum interturbat deque ea, si quid inquirere
curiosius voles, sat tibi, lector, habeto Graecum
Favorini librum, qui Omnigenae historiae
superscribitur. Illic etiam generis Alexandri
inveneris seriem, cui generi principium praestitisse
ferunt Oceanum vel Thetidem, exinque fluxisse per
Acrisium Danaumque atque Persea multosque alios in
Perdiccae genera vel Philipporum. Nam ne Olympiadi
quidem secus propago generosa est, cui deligentia pari
a mundi principio per Saturnum atque Neptunum, tum
etiam Telemona seriem generis attexuit, ad tertiumque
Neoptolemum docet prosapiam defluxisse, cuius uxor
Anasafia mater Olympiadis cluit. Igitur ad Alexandrum
mens recurrat.

Erat quidem ille ad omnes litteras iam peritus, et
sibi quisque ludus in puero imperiale aliquid fuerat

136

was laid on the ground, promptly followed the movement
of the earth, the cracking of thunder, the blowing of
the wind, the flash of the lightning, so that you might
see that concern for the entire world was involved with
his birth. Therefore Philip said apologetically, "I
must confess that I had not planned to raise the child
you bore, since it was not from my seed; but since I
perceive that it is divine progeny, I yield to your
prayers that it be brought up; and in memory of that
son who was born to me from an earlier marriage, now
resting in his grave, I shall give this one the name
Alexander."

7.   So the boy was reared excellently in royal
style.   All of Macedonia and Thrace as well as Pella
flocked to the official ceremony in his honor.   As he
grew up, his appearance was completely unlike
Philip's, nor did he resemble his mother.   He was also
unlike the one from whose seed he had sprung, but he
was very handsome in his own fashion, with curly golden
hair like a lion's mane, beautiful eyes, the right
pupil black and the left one blue-grey like the sky;
he was as spirited as a lion (that was plain to see).
So he grew with prudence, wisdom, and majesty to equal
his physical beauty.   His nurse was Alacrinis, his
pedagogue Leonides; Polynices, his instructor in
reading and writing, Alcippus of Lemnos in music,
Menicles of the Peleponnesus in geometry, Anaximenes of
Lampsacus in oratory; in philosophy, to be sure, his
teacher was the famous Aristotle of Miletus.

About Miletus, indeed, it is too long a story to
recount here, especially in view of this fact, that if
you would like to inquire more closely, reader, it
would suffice for you to have the Greek book of
Favorinus, which is entitled a universal history.
There, to be sure, you will find Alexander's whole
family tree, of which they say that Ocean and Thetis
were the founders in the beginning, and from them there
had flowed forth through Acrisius and Danaus, Perseus
and many others into the stock of Perdiccas and of
Phillippus.   Indeed, no less also for Olympias is the
ancestry noble, for whom, with equal care from the
world's beginning through Saturn and Neptune, Telemona
fashioned the stem of the race, and it teaches us that
Neoptolemus had flowed forth for the third generation,
and his wife Anasafia was called the mother of
Olympias.   Therefore our thoughts return to Alexander.

He was even at this time skilled in all branches of
letters, and every game was some kind of preparation

meditamentum. Nam sicubi tempus cum labore lectionis
absolverat, et iudicare solitus inter aequaevos et
industriari, quatenus inter hos argumenta iurgii
nascerentur; ac tunc alteri iurgantium favens, ubi
partem illius ingenio sublevasset, solitus in
contrariam resultare rursusque contra eam, cui paullo
ante patrocinatus fuerat, dicere. Itaque cum saepe
utrique parti utilis favisor ac strenuus victor foret,
opinionem non frustra sibi spectabilis ingenii
confirmarat. Interea viri, qui Philippi armenta vel
equitia curabant, equum spectabilis formae
pulchritudine absolutum regi deducunt aiuntque illum
armenti quidem regalis genus, formatum pedibus ad
Pegasi fabulam opinabilem, et si equi fuisse Laomedonti
eiusmodi praedicantur. Nec secus senserat Philipus.
Nam et actu corporis et linea pulchritudinis movebatur.
Sed addit equisius: 'Haec quidem, o rex, sunt in hoc
equo talia; sed est ei vitium beluile, namque homines
edit et in huiuscemodi pabulum saevit.' Et 'Heu,' rex
ait, 'numnam illud in isto proverbium est, quod semper
propter rebus bonis deteriora conlimitant? Enimvero
quoniam deductus semel, claudi eum atque ali curabitis,
sub claustris scilicet praeferratis. Quisque enim
subcubuerit legibus tristioribus, huiuscemodi melius
obiectabitur lanienae.' Et haec quidem rex, et cum
dicto iussa complentur.

Sed interea Alexander iam annum duodecimum
adpellens et comes patri fiebat et usu armorum indui
meditabatur, simulque cum exercitibus visi gaudebat et
equis insiliens et reliqua omnia miles ut poterat, adeo
ut Philippus haec demirans sic ad illum: 'O puer, aveo
quidem et vultu fruens et moribus tuis, eorumque aliud
duco ad similitudinem nostri, aliud vero auctius, quam
ut sit ex nostra natura. Sed nunc mihi ad proximam
usque iter est civitatem.'

8. Quod dictum cum Olympias etiam usurpasset
profectusque Philippus foret non simili adfectu quo
solitus, Nectanabum protinus repetit eumque consulit
super clandestino mariti consilio. Qui cum adsidente
sibi Alexandro ex arte illa astrica loqueretur,
interpellat puer et 'Heus tu,' inquit, 'istaene, quas
stellas appellas, agitant nunc in coelo ibique
visuntur?' Et Nectanabus ita esse respondit. Pergit
igitur Alexander: 'Possumne istas videre atque oculis
usurpare?' Adnuit posse. Tempus exigit. Vesperam

for empire, even in his boyhood. For whenever he had completed his reading assignments, he used to act as judge among his contemporaries and was actively involved when quarrelsome disputes arose among them; and then after favoring one or two other of the disputants, sustaining this side of the case by his own abilities, he would suddenly take the opposite position and speak against the one he had been defending shortly before. And so, since he was often a ready advocate and prompt victor on either side, he strengthened his reputation for spectacular abilities, not in vain for him. Meanwhile, the men who were taking care of Philip's herds and horses conducted to the king a horse perfect in the beauty of its splendid form and they said that its stock was of the royal herd, with its feet shaped as in the conjectural fable of Pegasus, and likewise they said that Laomedon's horses had been of this kind. Not otherwise was Philip's perception, for he was moved by the animal's beautiful lines and physical grace. But the trainer said in addition, "These qualities, O king, are indeed in this horse; but he has a bestial fault, in that he eats men and grows violent on food of this kind." "Alas," said the king, "is there not a proverb on that very point, that worse things always border on the good things? But now since the animal has once been led out, take care that he be confined and nourished, fettered with iron chains. For whoever falls under our harsher laws, by preference he will be thrown to this horse to be mangled." This is what the king said, and his orders were carried out to the letter.

Alexander was now twelve years old. He had become his father's companion and was studying military practice. He was happiest when with the army, leaping onto his horse and leaving all the other soldiers far behind, so that Philip, marveling at this, said to him: "My boy, I greet you as I enjoy both your countenance and your habits, some of them like to ours, others to be sure greater than would be from our nature. But now I must take the road to the next country."

8. After Olympias had taken cognizance of this statement and that Philip, having departed, would not be of as much influence as usual, Olympias promptly sought out Nectanabus and consulted him about the secret plan for her husband. Once, when he was talking about astrology with Alexander sitting close by, the boy interrupted saying, "You there, tell me, are those things you call stars moving, those stars that are visible in the sky?" And Nectanabus answered him in

139

pollicetur. Quae ubi advenerit, 'Comitare,' inquit,
'una mecum ad campestrem locum, easque tibi in coeli
choro lucentes ostendam.' Recipit ita sese facturum
velut cupidus puer. Ergo ubi tempus est, progressus
oppido dabat Alexandro videre, quae cupiverat. Enim
non una sedulitas discenti puero cum magistro. Namque
paulatim Alexander ad praescitum fossae praeceps
hominem adpellens impulsu improviso praecipitat;
ibique letali ictu cervicis Nectanabus adflictur haec
est conquestus: 'Mi,' inquit, 'fili, Alexander,
quodnam huius facti tibi consilium fuit?' At ille
respondit: 'Conquerendum igitur tibi est de arte ista,
quam noveras. Quippe nescius, quae te impenderent
humi, rimare ea, quae caeli sunt.' Ad haec magus:
'Equidem,' inquit, 'Alexander, laesum me letaliter
sentio, sed profecto nulli mortalium contra fatum
permissa est fuga.' Tum ille: 'Cur istaec inquis?'
Respondit magus: 'Olim quippe per hanc scientiam
videram fatale mihi fore a filio interfectu iri. Ea
igitur praescita non effugi.' Et Alexander: 'Anne ego
sum filius tuus?' Ita esse confitetur et fabulae
reliquam subserit seriem, tum Aegypti fugam tum
ingressum ad Olympiadam, et tractatum et amorem, et
quanam arte potitus uxore sit ad similitudinem dei. Et
in his dictis animam exaestuat. Hinc Alexander
comperto eo, quod pater sibi, quem interfecerat, fuit,
metuit eum in illo defosso insepultum et praedam
bestiis derelinqui. Nam et nox erat et secreta, quo
venerant. Naturali ergo monitus adfectu superponit
hominem humeris quam valentissime et revectat in
regiam. Ut autem reversus ad matrem est, cuncta
narrat, quae sibi supremo conloquio pater dixerat. Hoc
demirata est mulier et secus de se quam voluerat
iudicavit, quod tot annis vanis scilicet artibus lusa
probram rem fecerat. Nihilominus et sepelit cum decore
Nectanabum, et ut patri filius, sepulchrum erigit
operosissimum. Fuitque inde praenosse, quid huic
genito ad vitae clausulam deberetur: cum Nectanabus
Aegypto oriundus in Macedonia sit sepultus,
tantumdemque spatii e diverso Alexander, rex Macedonia,
morte sua foret Aegypto traditurus.

the affirmative. Then Alexander continued. "Can I see them with my eyes?" He answered that he could. When evening came, Nectanabus said, "Come along with me to a field where I can show you the stars shining in a heavenly circle." The boy was eager to do this, so leaving the city, Nectanabus provided Alexander the opportunity to see what he had desired.

And that was not the only thing the boy learned with this teacher. Somewhat later, Alexander, when standing at the edge of a deep trench, driven by a sudden impulse, pushed his teacher headlong into it. Nectanabus, with a lethal wound on his head, asked, "My son, Alexander, what was your reason for this deed?" The young man replied, "You should find that out yourself from your prophetic skill. For surely, if you don't know what's going to happen on earth, you couldn't investigate the things in heaven." To this the magician said, "Alexander, I perceive that I am fatally wounded, and this only proves that no man can ever escape his fate." Alexander asked, "Why do you say that?" The sorcerer answered, "Once upon a time, by means of my learning, I received a vision of my fate, namely, that I would be killed by my own son. This, therefore, as was foretold, I could not escape." And Alexander asked, "Am I your son?" Nectanabus confessed that it was so, and added the rest of the story--the flight from Egypt, his audience with Olympias, his falling in love with her, and the magic by which he possessed her in the likeness of a god. With these words he departed this life.

When Alexander discovered thus that it was his own father whom he had killed, he was afraid to leave him unburied in the ditch, a prey for wild beasts. For it was night, and a lonely place where beasts could come. Moved by natural feeling, he covered the body with earth as much as he could and rode back to the palace. When he saw his mother, he told her the whole story, including his father's last words.

Olympias marveled at this, especially that she had been tricked into immoral conduct for so many years through magic. Nonetheless she had Nectanabus buried with honor, and his son, as is proper, erected an expensive monument at his grave. From this it was foretold what would happen to his son at the end of his life: since Nectanabus was born in Egypt but buried in Macedonia, likewise, many years later Alexander, king of Macedonia, would meet his own death in Egypt.